T0196077

Also by Charles L. Roe

Moonbeams and Mistflowers
Cumberland
My Native Home
Thistles
Barren River

Adrift

iUniverse, Inc.
New York   Bloomington

ADRIFT

A Memoir

Copyright © 2009 by Charles L. Roe

All rights reserved. No part of this book may be used or reproduced by any means, graphic, electronic, or mechanical, including photocopying, recording, taping or by any information storage retrieval system without the written permission of the publisher except in the case of brief quotations embodied in critical articles and reviews.

iUniverse books may be ordered through booksellers or by contacting:

iUniverse
1663 Liberty Drive
Bloomington, IN 47403
www.iuniverse.com
1-800-Authors (1-800-288-4677)

Because of the dynamic nature of the Internet, any Web addresses or links contained in this book may have changed since publication and may no longer be valid. The views expressed in this work are solely those of the author and do not necessarily reflect the views of the publisher, and the publisher hereby disclaims any responsibility for them.

ISBN: 978-1-4401-1479-3 (pbk)
ISBN: 978-1-4401-1481-6 (cloth)
ISBN: 978-1-4401-1480-9 (ebk)

Printed in the United States of America

iUniverse rev. date: 2/17/2009

Adrift

A Memoir

By

Charles L. Roe

For Juanita, whose hand lay firmly on my arm for our stroll through life, and for Lynn and Larry and the grandkids – this is the way it was one summer long ago.

Rejoice, o young man ... in the days of thy youth, while the evil days come not, nor the years draw nigh...

— Ecclesiastes 12.1

Strange to wander in the mist, each is alone. No tree knows his neighbor. Each is alone.

— Herman Hesse

Re-creating something in words is like being alive twice.

— Ancient Chinese Poet

Foreword

Our family must depend on old stories told and hearsay, on old photographs faded and badly annotated, and on hazy memories that mix fable and fact, to tell you about the Roes. The current generation is interested in all this history, but the oldsters have mostly died out now without passing much information on. And it is painstakingly difficult and uncertain to track down the facts now when just a few years ago some of these people were living and could have been asked. The Roes don't seem to have been exceptional people, but on the other hand they left a comfortable land to settle on two frontiers – the Maryland eastern shore in the 1660's and the Kentucky Licking River Valley in the late 1790's.

Family members who have traced them have found few records except for the usual papers on birth, marriage, land ownership, taxes, and death. Although the family's roots in Suffolk County, England are well established and we see a Thomas Roe living there in the early 1600's, it is his son, also named Thomas, who left there sometime in the 1650's that we are first interested in. Why he left green England's shores to face the hazardous sea crossing and an unknown future is lost in the mists of time. But he apparently reached the seaport of Norfolk and lived there for a few years, marrying, and then moving his family to Queen Anne's County on the Maryland eastern shore. Several generations of Roes are documented to have lived there. A community still exists today named "Roe" and is on all state highway maps.

But sometime in the 1790's a son of the line, James, moved to Bath County, Kentucky and took as his bride one Abigail Mershon from nearby Fleming County. Abigail was from a well-to-do family and could trace her ancestry back to Dutch Burghers of the 1500's. Their sixth and seventh children were twins – Carline Cofax and Cornelius born in 1816. Cornelius married Jane Ewing around 1850 and they moved to a property near the Fleming-Nicholas County line where Buchanan Creek converges with the Licking River.

Cornelius prospered as a farmer but this was a few years after he had taken time off to go and get himself involved in the Mexican War. He served with some distinction, and whether or not he ever reached the rank of Colonel or Brevet Colonel, he was so-styled for the rest of his days. As he approached doddering old age, he became a colorful figure on the streets of Flemingsburg wearing a bright red cape with his military sword buckled about his waist.

He was buried in a little family cemetery on his property near Pleasant Valley that will probably be forgotten after this generation. His farm was divided into parcels for each family member. These were too small to provide sufficient acreage for tobacco, hay, hemp, and corn and over the years each surviving child sold his or her share to outsiders. Cornelius and Jane's marriage was blessed with three children before she died and Cornelius remarried a Stanfield. The second of his children by Jane Ewing was Filmore Millard Roe.

Filmore married a twin girl – America Emmaline Longbottom – and the Scots-Irish ancestry was introduced into the family. They had seven children. Exigent photographs show a mustachioed man with an almost dwarfish woman – she dressed in cotton with a sunbonnet. They purchased another property on Buchanan Creek not far from Filmore's boyhood home. His farm was successful, but he had three sons to help him run it. The two eldest sons – Cornelius and Lilburn – were named for their grandfathers. All the children were sent to get some schooling. His youngest son, and my father, William Jesse, attended for three years. Later in life he had to solve problems with simple division and multiplication. He turned complex problem solving over to his children. Although he was an avid newspaper reader, he was a poor writer. He usually paid off his work-hands with cash. When he was forced to give a check, he had a trustworthy one fill in the numbers after which he would laboriously write his signature.

Filmore's children attended school – the girls received more schooling than the boys who were needed in the crops. They attended church at the Mt. Tabor Methodist, where several of the family members lie buried today. They bought some supplies in the town of Licking which had two stores and a post office. Licking was where the Abners Mill-Licking Road split with one branch going out to Cowan and the other, whereon Filmore lived, going around by Pleasant Valley out to the Carlisle-Flemingsburg Road.

My father recalled the hard farm life. All work was done with horse or mule. Nothing was electrified. You went to bed when it got dark and you arose well before daylight to get milking and hog-feeding chores out of the way so you could be in the fields at dawn. When later in life we had electric in our barns and could strip tobacco on gloomy days, he remarked that it was fortunate that the old-time farmers did not have electricity or they would have worked themselves to death toiling far into the night. He remembered the tobacco wars of the early part of the century when the buyers banded together to set ridiculously low prices and the farmers retaliated by holding out their tobacco, and burned the barns of those who refused to do likewise. In those days tobacco warehouses were found in every small town. Farmers had to bring their crops in by wagon. When trucks were available for transport, the warehouses concentrated in the main towns – that is – the county seats.

Still, the family usually got to town on Saturday evening for shopping and the kids maybe got to go to the Flickers. As they got older there were parties and dances. My father was known in his younger days as Willie and was noted to be something of a gay blade (before it had homosexual connotations) and was in much demand at these affairs. It is interesting that he loved music and dance, but did a one-eighty with his children discouraging us from any of these time-wasting pursuits. I think of all the nights on the farm when we could have been learning to play guitar or banjo.

But this story is not about Willie Roe. Though his story may be as interesting as his son's who the subject is. W.J. as he was known in later life, married Nannie Jones, the sister of his brother's wife. His own sister married her brother. Thus, I had numerous double cousins – kin both through my mother and father to them. W.J. worked for years on the L & N Railroad in a maintenance section gang and later at an oil refinery. He and his growing family were living in Covington in 1933 when the great depression roared in. His wages dropped as food supplies in stores dwindled. He determined that he could farm and do better. At least he could raise vegetables and fruit for canning and feed his family.

So he moved to a farm on the Harrison-Bourbon County line where I was born in 1934. My father – a rabid Cincinnati Reds baseball fan – followed all the major league teams. In 1934 a young fireballer named Lynwood Thomas "Schoolboy" Rowe was smoking hot for Detroit of the American League setting a record with sixteen straight wins. When I was born in December he decided to name me after him. Regrettably, he had an Uncle Thomas of whom neither he nor my mother was fond. They tried other names in combinations and finally named me Charles Lynwood, but determined to call me Lynwood. However, through my young years I never heard that name as my next oldest sibling decided the family should call me Snookie after our cat.

But all that will come out later. Here I am trying to wrap up the family history. W.J. was a heavy smoker. He died early – at 57 – of heart failure the certificate said, but he spent his last days in an oxygen tent from the effects of emphysema. His wife outlived him by 36 years and might have lived to be a hundred if it were not for an incompetent small town doctor. Of their eight children, six lived to adulthood and five married. They have so far produced only one male great-grandchild to W.J. who bears the Roe name.

Chapter 1

The big bus roars out the new four-lane road that Governor Chandler had caused to be built between Lexington and his hometown of Versailles. The beautifully landscaped horse farms with their blooded stock grazing in the well-tended fields slide by the window as I watch and worry and try not to miss anything. The trip to Louisville takes less than two hours and the bus makes several stops along the way to pick up additional passengers. The driver is making time while he can. This is the only stretch of four-lane road he will encounter until he reaches the environs of Louisville.

Juanita had brought me to Paris to catch the bus on the second Sunday in May. I have to get to Louisville and find a place to stay tonight for I will start work at the Jones-Dabney Paint Company in the morning. I could probably have gotten Clyde to take me to Paris, but he was still grousing about me leaving the farm and leaving the crop for him to raise and leaving Mom in his care. I had stayed on a year after high school. Mom didn't pay me anything for tending her part of the crop. She gave me a couple dollars on Saturday when we went to town. When I wanted to buy Juanita a present for Christmas or her birthday, I had to go to Mom and ask her for the money. It wasn't her fault. She didn't have much money. I would have given anything if, after high school, I could have gone on to college, but we didn't have the money. It wasn't in the cards. I was going to rot in Nicholas County. Clyde and I would wind up old bachelors sharing a house.

Then on my last day of school I had my first date with Juanita. She was my first girlfriend. We met on Saturdays at the movie in Paris and later I got my driver's license and drove over to her house on Oxbow Hill and picked her up during the week. Sometimes we went to the movie and sometimes we just parked and talked and kissed. She was a year behind me in school so it worked out all right that I stayed the extra year on the farm taking care of the crop for Mom while we were going together and she was finishing up.

The summer before she had worked in Lexington and I thought that would not be too bad. We would see each other on the weekends and maybe I could drive up there sometimes. But she had other things planned. She wanted to get far from the farm. She had applied for the FBI in Washington, but she wasn't waiting to see whether or not that job would materialize. She talked about leaving as soon as graduation was over and going to Louisville or Cincinnati. She pulled me along in her planning. I was lukewarm to the idea. It was comfortable on the farm, and I was reluctant to leave and face the uncertainty of life in the city. But she prevailed and we had driven down there the week before and found jobs. I had to report on Monday. She would come on in two weeks after graduation.

Until last week, I have never been farther along this road than Frankfort, and that only on a couple class trips. Louisville had seemed a nice town when I was there except that I was under some stress trying to find employment in the few hours we had there. I had gotten something. It was called a mail clerk for the company, but it seemed like a glorified office boy. And the pay was not much. Maybe I could either find something better or transfer elsewhere in the plant when I got there. At least I wouldn't be stuck behind a desk all day.

As the bus rambles along, I reflect that I am making a dramatic change in my life. I am leaving eighteen years on the farm. I am leaving all the touchstones of my memory. I have pushed away from a known shore into uncharted waters. Everything I am – everything I know – is rooted in those Bluegrass hills. They are deep in the fabric of my being. I am not at all sure that I can endure away from their nurturing touch.

One of my earliest remembrances is of the time my father took my brother, Jim, and me to see his Uncle Harlan just before his death. Uncle Harlan died in 1937 so I had to be just two years old then. I don't remember much that was said, but the whole event made a strong impression on me that stayed with me all my life.

Uncle Harl, as he was called, had been the dominant patriarch of his generation. My grandfather's sons had worked for Uncle Harl, he had been the one they looked to for advice and who they would have gone to for approval of business ventures, marriages, or employment. In his younger days my father had spent considerable time at his home and was as close to his cousins as he was to his own brothers and sisters.

The day before we go to see Uncle Harlan, Pop takes Jim and me to town and buys us matching suits. They are what we call sun suits in those days, but they are simply one-piece short-legged suits that you get into like coveralls. We wear them with long socks because it is getting into the fall of the year. My mother, sisters, and older brothers do not accompany us. Just my father, Jim, and myself riding out the unfamiliar road that goes to Winchester and turning off somewhere. Later I think that the reason must have been that Uncle Harlan has never seen my brother and me, and my father either wants Uncle Harlan to see us or us to see him before he dies.

We enter the darkened sitting room and Uncle Harlan lies in a very high bed that I can barely see above. The thing that strikes me strange is that there are no women in the room. There is a stove with a fire going and eight or ten men sitting about the room, all wearing dress coats, and all mute. No one speaks to my father other than the man who opened the door, although all seem to nod recognition to him. I know no one in the room although I suppose these are my father's cousins.

We remove our coats and they are laid in a chair because we are to stay for only a moment. Our father pushes us forward to the edge of the bed and the only words I specifically remember being spoken is Pop saying, "Uncle Harl, these are my boys." We stand silently for his consideration. We are both shy in company and particularly among strangers. And we are always afraid of displeasing my father who is a strict disciplinarian.

Uncle Harl, apparently in great pain, gives us a brief appraisal and tries to speak to Pop ending his attempt with a moan. We are there but briefly and then a silent ride back home. Pop seems to be preoccupied and I make the judgment then that I later verify that Uncle Harlan's death is a great personal loss to him.

We enter Louisville along Breckinridge Street and cut across to Broadway and pull into the Greyhound station near Fifth Street. I reach into the overhead and drag down the old pressboard suitcase that Mom and Pop had bought Jimmy when he went on his Junior trip at school and that I had used for my two class trips as well. It is already getting dingy where we have stored it in the junk room upstairs. It is a small suitcase but easily contains the few articles of clothing I have brought along.

I move out onto the sidewalk and am lost. My vague plan is to try to find a room. Something that can be rented by the week or month. Failing that, I will stay the night at the YMCA and maybe the people at my work will be able to point me to something tomorrow. I wander disconsolately along the sidewalk moving away from the center of town toward the residential area. But here are row houses with businesses on the first floor – pawnbrokers and thrift stores. It seems like a poor part of town.

A black panhandler stops me and asks for money. I shake my head and try to move on but he presses me. I tell him I don't have any money to spare, thinking of the twenty dollars or so I have in my pocket, the proceeds from cashing in the defense bond I got during the war with my dimes buying a stamp every week. I tell him I have to move on. I am looking for a room for the night. He says he knows just what I want and urges me to follow him. We move along the street to where a large corpulent man is standing outside one of the row houses talking to another man. The black man steers me to him and starts to chatter about having brought him business and expecting a reward. The man eyes me coldly.

"You looking for a room?"

The house does not look at all reputable. "Yes. I'm looking."

"Well, I have nice rooms upstairs. I can let you have one for seven dollars a week. You want to look?"

"Since I'm here." I don't want to have a confrontation, but I don't like this part of town. I follow him up a flight of stairs.

"Here it is. A fine room."

It is a nice room in appearance, but there is a bad odor about the place. Like beneath the paint is decades of dirt and scum and rot and old mouse droppings and cockroach shells.

"It is nice, but I really wanted something closer to my work."

"Where's that?"

"Out at Twelfth and Hill."

"Walk down here to Twelfth and Broadway. Bus takes you right there."

I start to feel threatened, but there is no way I am going to lodge here. "I don't think so. I'll look around some more."

He again eyes me coldly. "Why were you walking around with that bum?"

"He just latched onto me. Started out asking me for money."

"Well, run him off. He'll rob you if he gets the chance."

We come back on to the street. The Negro is waiting.

"You see, young man. Didn't I tell you he had good rooms? Reasonable, too."

The big man raises his hand threateningly. Maybe he is mad that he hasn't rented the room. "Get the hell away. Don't come around here again."

He steps away tentatively. "Didn't I bring you trade?" he whines. "Ain't no way to treat me."

"Get on away. I'm looking for a patrolman."

"Ain't right. Ain't right to treat me thisaway." He shuffles on down the street.

The big man regards me considering what else he might say. Finally says, "You better be getting down for the night. Go up to the YMCA at Second Street. They give you a clean bed in the dormitory for a dollar or two. Don't have to worry about your things getting stolen."

"Okay. I think that's what I'll do."

He watches me walk away. Calls after me. "And don't talk to bums on the street. They are after your money or more."

From 1937 until 1944 we live as tenants on a farm owned by the Lebus brothers, Clarence and Frasier, on the Winchester Road, just outside Lexington. The farm is formerly a racehorse farm that has fallen on hard times during the depression and the Lebuses have bought the two hundred acres cheap with the idea of farming it and waiting for a chance to turn a good profit on it. How it has come to its low state I couldn't say, but it is nestled in among some of the Bluegrass's prime real estate. It is just across the road from John E. Madden's palatial Hamburg Place where Derby winners are bred and young tanned men play polo in the carefully coiffured pastures on Sunday afternoons.

The farm has three tobacco barns and a racehorse barn. A training track for thoroughbreds has been carved out in a valley below the horse barn and runs through trees and across a fill. The racehorse barn is the sturdiest structure on the place and during the war we actually board workers in the stalls.

The house where we live is an ante-bellum mansion that has been allowed to run down. Along one fence are the foundations of slave cabins. The remains of two icehouses are also in evidence. A great upping stone sits prominently in the front yard. The front porch is pillared but the floor has fallen in. A long back porch leads off to a cooking kitchen and washroom that is detached from the main house. In pre-Civil War days the food had been prepared in this wing and brought to the dining room. Now we have installed the kitchen where the earlier dining room had been.

We raise great crops of tobacco. Work hands in this depression time are easily found and cheap to employ. My cousins have gone into the CCC to save their parents the burden of having to feed and cloth them. My father lures them to the farm and pays them a small wage and gives them board. And they toil under the hot sun beside my brothers to bring in the great crops. Before the acreage controls are placed on at the beginning of the war, one year we raise 85 acres of burley. The three barns can't hold it. We take the excess to Lexington and hang it to dry in the Lebus Brothers' warehouse on Fourth Street.

My mother is as busy as my father during the intense times of tobacco housing. Sometimes we have a dozen men or more for dinner. My mother provides them beans, potatoes, ham, and sausage and heaping bowls of vegetables, gravy, and fluffy clabber milk biscuits that melt the rich cow's butter and then melt in your mouth. It is all accomplished on an old coal-fired cook stove. They eat hurriedly and rush back to the fields leaving their dishes to be washed and the next meal prepared, for many of them board overnight.

Jimmy and I are everywhere getting underfoot. We are given the chore of carrying water to the men in the field cutting tobacco and the men in the barn hanging it to cure. In these pre-school days everything is strange and exciting. We turn brown as toast under the warm Kentucky sun. We never dream it will all end.

I lie in the bed in the YMCA dorm and listen to my wind up alarm clock tick away the seconds and hours of the night. I have gone to the drugstore across the street from the YMCA and bought the clock so I won't oversleep in the morning and be late for my first day of work. Two other men have come in the room and slipped into their beds. I have given them my name but don't converse with them further. I listen to their conversation for a while till they grow bleary and drift away into deep noisy sleep. I worry that the alarm clock will not sound in the morning. I still worry that I will be robbed. I intend to sleep with my billfold under my pillow.

I worry about the job I will be starting tomorrow. Will the people be easy to work with? Will I have an understanding boss or someone who will be critical? My relatives in the auto plants in Cincinnati always complain about their bosses and foremen and how they are always being pressed to increase their output – to get more accomplished. Well, I'm not afraid of hard work, but I worry about making some mistake.

When I went to see about the job, it had been late on the day I had spent job-hunting. I was becoming frantic. I had come to see about another job at the same company – a clerk in their personnel department. But they told me they had just filled it. They still needed a mail clerk. I was put off by the little pay. Juanita was disgusted. She said I had to take something. She had already found a position. She darkly hinted that I was being stubborn and just didn't want to leave the farm.

I went back in and said I would take the test for the mail clerk position. Apparently, it was some standard test that evaluated how you did in high school. I didn't have much trouble with it. I waited while they checked my answers. One of the men suddenly exclaimed, "By God, he worked the square root problem."

They came together out of the front office to see me.

"Where were you before? You could have had the personnel clerk position. We don't have one applicant in ten who can extract a square root. You seem to have a good math background."

"If I take the mail clerk job, could there be a chance I could transfer somewhere else after a while?"

"Certainly. A lot of our people start at one job and work their way up. I think we have three or four former mail clerks working at other positions here now."

"Where is the one I am replacing going?"

"Oh, I believe he is going away to school in the fall. But he wanted to take the summer off. Luckily, he will have a week with you to show you the ropes."

The windows in the dormitory are cracked letting in a gentle breeze. Sleep will not come. I am too keyed up. Too worried that I will sleep and then oversleep. I think of the room I shared with Clyde back on the farm. We were both quiet sleepers. I look at the clock. Back on the farm they will soon be rising to eat breakfast and get the morning chores out of the way. Clyde will be getting the tobacco patch ready for planting and the canvas will be pulled back on the tobacco beds getting the young shoots ready for transplanting.

Like I have been – transplanted from my home to this place.

Chapter 2

I stand in the little store across the street and watch the early comers passing into the main building of Jones-Dabney. I have risen early and caught the bus down Broadway and connected to the one that runs out 12th Street. I have never ridden a city bus. I don't know to drop the coins down into the depository. The driver sizes me up and asks if I need a transfer. I tell him where I am going and he tears me off a transfer slip and tells me to give it to the driver on the connecting line.

I have left my suitcase behind at the Y. If I get a room near here, I will have to go all the way back down there this evening and bring it back. But I don't want to be lugging it around. I can cover a lot of ground, or sidewalk, when I am footloose. I sip an orange pop and eat a little pie I have bought for breakfast. Everything is expensive. I am going to have to watch my funds. I think of the big breakfast Mom will be fixing for Clyde and Colleen.

Fifteen minutes before the time I have been told to report, I walk across the street and approach the doors. A guard is standing there when I push inside. I tell him I am reporting for my first day of work and he directs me to a large glass window where two ladies sit at a switchboard just on the other side. I wait while the one closest to me finishes connecting a call. There is glass on the other side of the room as well and I can see that beyond that are two other offices with a bustle of activity. In one corner of the switchboard room is a boy about my age sorting mail.

The operator says hi and tells me her name is Aggie. She puts a call through to the Office Manager, Mr. Gerlach. He occupies a glass-enclosed office just on the other side of the switchboard room, and I see his secretary pick up the phone and look across at me when Aggie tells her who I am. I am sent around there to meet Mr. Gerlach and am given a bunch of forms to fill out. They are distressed that I can't fill in an address on the forms. They put them away and tell me to come in tomorrow and complete them when I have found a place to stay.

I am told that I will be paid twice a month and that I will be paid for overtime. That will help because I am making little enough. Typically, the mailboy works about ten hours each day picking up the mail at the post office when it opens and staying after the other office workers leave in the afternoon to get all outgoing correspondence into a nearby mailbox for a late afternoon pickup. They keep calling me the mailboy which doesn't sound nearly as grand as mail clerk.

I am ready to get started then and Madelaine, the secretary, takes me out to introduce me to the office staff. In the other office that I have seen works four young women, probably not more than two or three years older than me. They handle the company's accounts receivable and payable and the ordering of supplies and goods needed around the office and in other parts of the plant. I meet Aggie again and Pauline, the other switchboard operator. And then I am turned over to a freckled-face bundle of energy, Paul Schwab, the incumbent mail clerk who is stuffing mail into a compartmented satchel that he slings over his shoulder preparatory to distributing it around the plant.

He gives me a brief rundown of the routine. I am to bring the mail to this table in the switchboard room and sort it into piles. During the week I will learn how to place it because Mr. Gerlach comes looking for incoming checks and others will come by to pick up their mail and get started on the day's work. So I have to put it into piles where they can find it. On Mondays the mail is heavy, so it takes a long time to sort out what I pick up at the post office. I will only make one delivery run around the plant in the morning. On other days I will deliver twice in the morning and twice in the afternoon. After that, I will be busy getting mail together to go out at the end of the day. He shows me how to operate the big metering machine. About once a month I will have to take the mechanism to the post office and have postage added to the meter.

The plant is much larger than it appeared from outside the fence. The main building where we are has a large wing that runs back from the road. It is two stories and filled with offices. Several of these are occupied by salesmen and their secretaries. The shadowy salesmen are seldom in their offices. They are more often traveling about by rail visiting clients in various cities around the country taking orders for Devoe Paints which is our parent company. I can't fully grasp the organizational structure and what each office accomplishes, but they are a busy bunch. I think that we must be selling a lot of paint.

We start around the plant and I find that there are perhaps ten more buildings in all. One is a laboratory where they develop new kinds of paint and experiment with different ingredients and bonding agents to improve the texture and durability of the paint. There are buildings where the paint is actually produced and put into buckets and drums. The drums are huge 55-gallon affairs and are manhandled about by a crew of mostly black laborers.

At lunchtime Paul takes me to the canteen. A man called Pop and his son are in white cook hats and forking out hotdogs and making up sandwiches. I order up a hotdog. Paul tells me it will be a dime but I can get two for fifteen cents. I am ravenous. I buy two and a chocolate milk. It is the first time I have ever seen milk in a paper carton.

I tell Paul of my need to find a room and we pour over the ads in a paper that one of the guys has. He circles two or three that are in convenient locations and says that I should leave right after work and try to be first to them. There will be plenty of time later in the week for him to show me how to get the mail out.

You know how those things get started. A bunch of men working in the field are always talking and arguing to pass the time. The work is routine and automatic after a while, and the talk takes your mind off your aching muscles and how long it is till dinnertime and how little the job is paying. Well, it is tobacco housing time and Jim and I are just little shavers tagging along with the men in the field, fetching sticks, gathering up broken leaves and putting them in a neat pile to spear them on a wire to take them to the barn to cure with the other tobacco. My older brothers work in the tobacco with my father and ten or twelve other hands. This is the pre-war years when we still grow the large crops without controls or government support.

I think it starts with Buddy Howard complaining about his aches and pains and everyone begins kidding him about how he is getting old and isn't good for anything except rocking on the front porch. They go on and on and Buddy gets ticked off and starts claiming that he is still as good as any of them and in a lot better shape for doing some things, and the outgrowth of the whole thing is he says he can beat any of them in a footrace. That gets the big ho-ho from everybody and they don't think he is serious until he imposes a few additional conditions. They are going to race from the house to the main highway and back, a distance of nearly two miles, and they are to do it barefoot. They talk about it all day and what grows out of it is a contest in which every man who wants to run puts in a dollar, winner take all, and my father is to be the judge. Some of the fellows aren't too crazy about running and tearing up their feet on the gravel and having to work the next day on sore feet, and that is Buddy's chance to give them the needle and egg them into running.

Well, it gets talked up so much everybody is keyed up and ready to go. They are all sitting on the back porch after supper letting the food digest and going over the rules. It is about dark and they figure that it just adds to the strangeness of the race. Then of all things to happen, Buddy is carrying water in from the pump for my mother and drops a bucket on his ankle. He is hopping around and moaning and takes the shoe off and they get his foot into a pan of cold water before it swells. They are all disappointed, but it is obvious that Buddy can't run. He wants them to call it off for about a week or so until he can run, but they decide to go ahead since everybody else is all set to go. So they strip off their shoes and my father sends them off in the dark. Half of them don't even make it through the barnlot. The big sharp gravel punches holes in the tender soles of their feet and they don't dare run in the grass, which has been cut for hay, and hides sharp stubble sticking up that can puncture right through your foot. So one by one they come limping back to where my father has thoughtfully provided a washtub of cold cistern water for them to bathe their feet.

It turns out that only my brother, Clyde, and one other work hand finishes the race with Clyde winning the ten dollars. Everybody's feet are in pitiful condition. Buddy is delighted every time he sees one of them straggling back. What a bunch of featherbrains, he cackles. What a bunch of sissies. They sit around the washtub soaking their dogs. They are not much in a mood for levity. They are thinking about having to work all day tomorrow on sore feet. They are still soaking them when Buddy dumps his pan of water and goes to bed. He is still chuckling amusedly. The next morning he is still laughing at all the hobbling and groaning. His ankle has come around pretty good. In fact, he is walking better than any of them. After that, he keeps challenging them to another run, but he can't get any takers.

The big house at 607 W. Ormsby Street belongs to Doctor Shaw. He and his wife live on the first floor. It is a three-story house. There are four bedrooms on the second floor and two more on the third floor. There are also two bathrooms on the second floor. Mrs. Shaw sees to the renting of the six rooms and collects the rent each week. A colored maid comes in each day and cleans and makes the beds and changes the sheets weekly. The maid is named Flora and she is as fussy about the rooms as if the house were hers. She lays down the law that I am not to sit or lie on or sleep under the bedspread. She fusses about the hygiene of the six male houseguests, and if you try her patience she will recommend to Mrs. Shaw that you be evicted.

The room rents for ten dollars a week. That is more than I can afford on my slight salary. The two third floor rooms are seven dollars, but neither is available. My room is at the front of the house looking out on Ormsby and a block south I can see the corner of Central park. The lot around the Shaws' house is filled with big shade trees. Ormsby ends a block to the west and we have little foot or automobile traffic going past. I am given my own passkey and told that noise will not be tolerated. I have brought Clyde's old military radio with me and got it repaired and listen to it sometimes at night. Mostly to the Louisville Colonels baseball games. I keep it low and never receive any complaints.

The location of the house is ideal for me. I can walk south in the morning. I cut through Central Park and pass through St. James Court on my way down to the post office at Fifth and Lee Street where I pick up the mail. I carry it back to Hill Street and I stand out waiting on a bus. But usually some people on the way to work spot me and pull over, and I jump in with the mailbag.

In the afternoons I walk back from work down Hill Street and turn at Seventh to come into the house from a different direction. When I enter in the afternoon, I check the table just inside the door to see if any mail has arrived for me. Sometimes Mrs. Shaw will call to me from the adjoining living room where she is watching TV. One afternoon after I have just begun rooming there I find her watching the coronation of Queen Elizabeth. I don't think it is live but it might have been. Sent by cable somehow maybe. The picture is washed out and grainy. It is fantastic to see the girl that I have seen in the papers and newsreels during the war being crowned. She looks scared and vulnerable. No matter who you are sometimes you find yourself in circumstances that overwhelm you.

15

Now that I am settled in, Paul wants to take me out to see some of the town. He has a car and we talk about going to a ballgame, but we settle for driving around and we spot a carnival. We walk around looking at the rides, and I go on one or two things with him. I am still conserving my money. Payday is not until the end of the month. I am glum because it is May 19th, the anniversary of my first date with Juanita. We have planned to be together, but it won't happen this year.

There is a wheel of chance and Paul puts down a nickel. He urges me to do the same. I drop one on number 19. The wheel spins and stops on my number. The guy looks at me funny and hands me a tin box of English toffee. There is a picture of Queen Elizabeth in her robe and crown. It is a memento of the coronation. I take the box and move on. The guy wants me to play some more.

That Buddy Howard is a card all right. Most workers you get on the farm are hangdog types who inure themselves to hard labor and do their work quietly and not always efficiently and are used to the boss's insinuations and criticisms. Now Buddy isn't like that at all. Criticism just runs off him like rain. He never loses his humor and is something of a prankster to boot. He is some kind of a distant relative and Pop always gets him to help us at tobacco housing time. Us kids are crazy about him and always hang around him when we can. He ends up entertaining us, making cornstalk fiddles or telling us outrageous fibs until Pop chases us away so he can get Buddy back to work.

The last year before the war Buddy is helping us and dreams up his top practical joke. My two older brothers are big enough to help in the crop. Odell works in the barn and Clyde is a cutter working in the field. Both of them have smoked for years, but they keep it from Pop. Of course, I'm sure he knows about it already. Pop doesn't miss much. Odell and Clyde figure he probably knows about it too, but they still ditch their butts when they see him coming.

Well, Buddy is driving one of the wagons. You know, picking up the green tobacco in the field and taking it to the barn, passing it up to the fellows to hang it on rails for curing, and going back to the field for another load. What he does is to go in the barn and tell the men working there, including Odell, a cock and bull story about how Pop has caught Clyde smoking in the field and has taken a tobacco stick and beat him half to death. Buddy is very convincing and tells it in a distressed and agitated manner elaborating on all phases of the beating, adding much color and description, calling out the men who have come to Clyde's aid and pulled his irate father away before the beating can become fatal. Everyone in the barn is thunderstruck and Odell is so concerned for his brother that he has to come down out of the barn with the shakes. Buddy is so elated by his success that he goes back to the field and tells the same story to Clyde and the field hands using Odell as the victim.

Now both groups of men are equally concerned and, of course, they can't get together until after work when they can swap stories and the whole farce will be uncovered. Then Buddy will have his big laugh and everybody will laugh at the clever way he has pulled it off. Only trouble is he has made the story too good with no element of doubt left in anyone's mind. The work hands won't meddle in, but among the field hands is my Uncle Lilburn. He is seething and the next time Pop, who is driving the other wagon, comes to the field Uncle Lilburn climbs him. Uncle Lilburn has hold of Pop's shirt when a look at his blank stare of innocence reveals in a flash their gullibility. Uncle Lilburn, Odell, and Clyde are mad as hell at Buddy and Buddy tells everybody he is sorry. You can't stay mad at Buddy for long. Pop thinks it is hilarious and he laughs and laughs. He tells the story over and over all through the war years when Odell and Clyde are away in the South Pacific. And he always gets Buddy to help in the housing during the war when help is hard to find. But Buddy never reforms and he somehow makes the backbreaking housing work something to look forward to and fun while we are doing it.

On Friday Paul leaves early, and I am on my own. I get the mail out and start thinking about what I will do on my free weekend. On the next weekend I am going home and Juanita will be coming back with me. Now I want to get downtown as well as to explore all the streets around where I live. I got here the week after the Kentucky Derby. They say that the town was a madhouse and a moving party during Derby week, but I will have to wait a full year to find out about that.

Lower Fourth Street between Broadway and the river is a spectacle of flashing neon and moving bodies on Saturday night. The seven or eight movie houses fill to capacity. The little restaurants that border the street and the bars catch patrons flitting between department stores and theaters. The Taylor Drug store on the corner of Walnut has people waiting for a seat at the soda fountain. Record stores broadcast the latest hits out onto the street. The ten-cent stores cater to the thrifty conscious. Movies play end to end. You can walk in anytime and stay to see the feature as many times as you want.

At the lower end of the street the neon dies down. and you can look out over the river at Jeffersonville and New Albany on the Indiana side of the river. A long highway bridge runs across from Second Street, and a railroad bridge is adjacent to it. Buses run over there, and a sidewalk runs along the side of the auto bridge for the hardy walker. It is surprising that at almost any time you will see people on the bridge.

The walk up to the commercial area of Fourth Street from my room on Ormsby is a long one. But I usually walk it to save the fifteen cents bus fare (if you buy tokens, they are two for a quarter). When I get to Louisville this spring, I have something wrong with my foot. It is painful to walk, but during the summer, probably because of all the walking, it gets better and the pain goes away. In these days, just off the farm, I can walk all day long. It doesn't bother me and I never tire. I like to walk along and hum or sing to myself and look at the houses and the flowers. On the walk down Fourth, I pass by some apartment houses and out front is parked a little black MG. I think it is the neatest car I have ever seen. I wonder if I will ever have one.

I go in an Orange Julius and have a glass of orange juice. It tastes watered down, but the hotdog is good. I find a little shopping center nearer my house at Second and Oak. There is a Taylor Drug there where I eat nearly every night. Next door to it is a little restaurant that has good milk shakes. Next to that is the Knox Theater that plays older movies and is cheap to get into. I watch the paper for movies that look good. I go at least once a week and sometimes more often.

I am already having a good time. It could be better if I had a better income. In any case, Juanita will be coming in a week. We will explore it together.

* * *

Jimmy and Snookie, 1937

* * *

Chapter 3

When I leave the house in the morning, the town is already astir. There is not much traffic on either Sixth Street or Ormsby, but I can hear the cars and big buses over on Fourth, the main artery for feeding traffic into downtown Louisville. I pass Magnolia Place and Floral Court (which some people call Floral Terrace) where Juanita will be living in a week's time and cross over at the corner into Central Park. Walkways run diagonally, and every other way through the park to spare the grass, and I follow them. A pair of tennis players is on the courts getting in an early set before work or school.

I follow beside the Romanesque colonnade and pavilion that is built down the center of the park and go down past the basketball courts that are not being used this early. I think that I will have to bring my basketball back the next time I go in to the farm. This would be a swell place to shoot goals. I think of all the old rusted hoops we had nailed on the corncrib or barns back on the farm. This will be real luxury playing on asphalt instead of packed earth. I always loved basketball and followed the University of Kentucky on the radio. I spent a lot of my time daydreaming of basketball and other sports. On the farm it gave me something to pass the time while I was doing mindless work. I need to put a lot of this kind of stuff behind me now.

I am also a Cincinnati Reds fan, but I notice that the paper here doesn't follow them. It is full of the Colonels, the Red Sox's AAA club. Maybe I can get out to Parkway Field to catch a game. Meanwhile they are on radio, and it is exciting to find an entirely new team to learn about. Listening to the radio you can forget they are just a minor league club. They have a lot of good players, it is said.

I cross from the park into St. James Court. It is a shaded street with big oaks growing along each sidewalk and a grassy divider in the center where people walk their dogs at morning. The imposing brownstone townhouses are named Belgravia and other exotic European names. One could almost fool himself on this street that he is in the heart of London or somewhere on the continent. You feel like you are in another city on this long block of houses. Who are these people who live in such houses? What kind of jobs do they hold? Maybe the houses are cut up into one-floor apartments. Then maybe you could rent one floor for something like a hundred dollars a month. That is still a lot of money, but some people have jobs that allow them to afford such luxury. Or sometimes several girls get together and pool their assets and rent a place together and share everything. Men sharing an apartment is not as common because they do not like to cook or do housework. If an unmarried man and woman want to make an arrangement of some kind, they have to pose as married. No one will rent to an unmarried couple.

I come out onto Hill Street and turn left. I only have to go down one block and cross over to walk to the post office at Fifth and Lee. I have left in time to quickly grab an orange soda and doughnut at the little grocery store across the street. I eat hurriedly and watch the post office across the street. Other company mail clerks, or people expecting something to be waiting in their boxes, are lounging about the doors waiting for them to open for the day. When I see the doors unlocked and people flowing in, I finish my soda and place the bottle in a wooden carton. I say good day to the storeowner and join the flow of people into the post office. They know me by now, and I don't even have to tell them I am from Jones-Dabney. A box that they have used to drop our mail into is pushed through the door to me. They have thrown a heavy bag made of some rain-resistant tarpaulin-like material in with the mail, and I quickly stuff the letters and other correspondence inside. I will return the bag after noon when I come back to make a second pickup for the plant.

Now I sling the bag over my shoulder and hasten back up to Hill to catch a ride. I am still strong from the farm work and the mailbag is nothing. But I am a slim lad, barely more than 100 pounds, and people look at me pityingly. Sometimes I am offered a ride, but I have been told to not accept rides from strangers. There are checks and other important items in the mail, and I am responsible for them. In any case, I know that I will get a ride with someone from the plant as soon as I reach Hill Street. Before I even get there someone coming past looks down the street and sees me coming. They pull to the curb and wait for me.

Perry Brown comes to stay with us the first year we live on the Lebuses' farm. He is a young slim man, burned nearly black by the sun. He has left his home in Lewis County and has come to the Lexington area looking for work as a day laborer. He still has a mother in Lewis County and writes to her sometimes – a letter or two a year – and goes back to see her infrequently. He has to catch a bus to Maysville and then hitch a ride over to the Vanceburg area. But he doesn't talk much about his family or home. And after he comes to be with us, we keep him even when there is no work to do in the tobacco. There is plenty enough else to do, and he pitches in on all the chores around the farm. He and Pop come to some agreement on his year around pay.

He comes to be treated like any other one of the family. He bonds immediately with Clyde and Odell. He is about the same age as Odell, but he has been sheltered and is shy around people. I don't know how he has worked up the courage to come see about the job. Mom treats him like another one of her boys. He is included in on all our family functions.

We younger children go with Mom and Pop to Paris on Saturday afternoon, and when we get back, Pop gives the car to Clyde and Odell and Perry to go to Lexington. They like the bigger town. And they don't usually return until near midnight. Their routine is to pick out a good movie to go to and afterwards go to a restaurant or the Walgreen's Drug Store and have a hamburger. Then, if it is a warm night, they might stand out on the street and talk and watch the girls passing by.

One night in Walgreen's they are eating and notice a shy cute little girl on another of the seats at the fountain. She keeps her head down, but they notice that she keeps sneaking glances at them, Clyde in particular. Clyde is a curly-haired kid of nineteen and probably even more shy than she is. The three of them have already been to the movie, but they make it up among themselves that if Clyde will approach her and ask her to a movie they will pool their remaining assets and pay the admission. Egged on by the other two Clyde does just that and the girl accepts. Perry and Odell sit in the car and wait through the movie until the two of them come out. Perry and Odell gleefully tell the story on Clyde the next morning. But nothing comes of it. Clyde never seems particularly interested in girls. He never goes anywhere to meet any of them.

Odell and Clyde go into the army even before Pearl Harbor happens and both get shipped to the South Pacific. Perry fails the physical because of high blood pressure. He is called to come for an army physical three times as they keep lowering the standards throughout the war. The last time we are sure he will go, and Mom gives him a tearful goodbye. She thinks of him just as a son. She will probably want to put a star in her window for him. But that night he comes back across the hill with his little carpetbag in hand. He has flunked the physical yet again.

He is with us all throughout the war. He marries in 1944 and Pop gives him grief about taking such a young wife. But Wynona is a swell girl, and she and Perry are happy together. They are tenants on our farm at Miller Station for a while. Just after Clyde and Odell return from the army and everything is getting back to normal, Pop and Perry have a blowup about something and Perry and Wynona leave. But they come to Pop's funeral and our families become close again. They name their son after Pop and Clyde.

The four girls in the adjoining office use me as a foil. One is named Nancy and one is Virginia and there are two Joans. They love my naïveté and kid the socks off me. I take their ribbing with good grace and try to rib them back, but they are bright young career women. Both Joans are married. Nancy seems to have numerous boyfriends. Virginia is from Hazard and shares an apartment with some other girls near St. James Court. She dates one of the male workers over in the Research and Development building.

While I am sorting the mail, I talk with Aggie and Pauline. Pauline is excited because she has persuaded Mr. Gerlach to let her fill a job opening in the Accounting Department. She will be making more money and will have ordinary hours. One of the switchboard ladies has to come in early at mornings and the other has to stay late in the afternoon to take calls that fall a little outside of our actual working hours. There is no way to have a recording that tells people that you are not open yet. It would be poor public relations to have such a recording anyway. Aggie is trying to get her daughter hired on as Pauline's replacement.

I am starting to know everyone around the plant. I only have a few moments to stop for idle chatter. Sometimes just the time that it takes me to drop off and pick up the mail in the offices. Particularly, the women who work as secretaries for the salesmen who are always out of town seem lonely and hungry for human contact. They have to be there in case their bosses call in and to take calls from people who want to leave messages or have information for them. Mrs. Stevenson on the second floor is one of my favorites. She is silver haired and has been with Jones-Dabney for forty years.

Out in the plant proper I have learned all the paths around the place and know all the little labs and offices hidden away in the warren of buildings. I pick up a lot of gossip and find out who is dating whom, what aspirations these various people have, and problems of work and family. They are mostly all friendly. I keep my eyes and ears open and add to the knowledge I came to Louisville with.

At lunchtime I get my hotdogs and chocolate milk and go to the lab where Paul has first taken me. Six or seven of us assemble there every day for lunch including Jimmy from Shipping and Forrest who got the job in Personnel that I wanted. Forrest comes in for merciless kidding from Jimmy because he works with a man named Bob Carroll whom everybody agrees is homosexual. I have met Bob, and I think he is a nice guy and friendly to me. I have never heard of queers until I come to Louisville. Apparently they are more numerous than I could have imagined. I don't know what exactly they want from you, but I have apparently had a close call by not getting the personnel job. Being ignorant on the matter I would have been an easy conquest for Bob.

Jimmy also is popular with the girls around the plant, but he claims it is bad policy to date where you work. He has a lot of unflattering things to say about some of the girls. And he is unceasing in his criticism of a girl that one of the lunchtime guys is seeing. They are engaged and Jimmy tries to convince him the girl is too old, and she is marrying him out of desperation. I think she is a swell girl and that Jimmy has rocks in his head.

After lunch Virginia brings me a bag that has a deposit for the bank. I bundle up the few outgoing letters that I have received and catch the bus down Hill to 19th Street. This is the location of the bank that Jones-Dabney does business with. When I came to work I had to be bonded because I would be carrying company funds from time to time. Sometimes at the bank I pick up some petty cash, but mostly I only carry the checks that we have received and deposit them. They put the necessary receipts and slips in the little deposit bag, and I take them back and give them to Virginia. But first I have to go yet again to the post office.

The buses on Hill Street around midday only run once an hour. It is just a quirk of scheduling that one comes about the time I am walking into the bank, and I have a long wait for the next one to take me back down to the post office at Fifth. There are no stores around. Nowhere I can go to get a soda or a snack. I have to wait out by the curb. There is not even a bench, but I find a place to sit and watch the traffic on 19th Street. It is called the Dixie Highway and is the main road south to Nashville. It is pleasant sitting out in late spring. In the wintertime it will not be such a nice wait.

I wonder where all the cars are going. I have been south as far as Mammoth Cave, but never into Tennessee. Mammoth Cave and Washington were our Junior and Senior trips at school. I liked both places. I like the big towns I have seen – Cincinnati and Louisville. I love the song that is popular – "Far Away Places". I would like to see China and Siam and the European capitals. I have found Hemingway's *For Whom the Bell Tolls* on the reading table at my rooming house and have borrowed it to read. His descriptions of Spain make me want to see that country. Odell and Clyde had come back from the war and told me all about the South Pacific. Maybe I will travel to some of those places someday. For now I will have to be content to explore this little corner of Louisville.

Pop is something of a tyrant. The responsibility of a large family makes him tend to want to control the lives of the family members, and he is somewhat tight with money. While we live on Lebus's, Geneva is going to high school at Lafayette in Lexington. She has Mom dress me up one day and takes me to school with her. Jimmy is going to school by then, but he goes to sit with his friends on the bus. He and Geneva are always fighting. I get along fine with her. The bus picks up other kids along its route. Since I am not of school age yet, they all look like big kids to me – almost adults. A boy gets on and sits by Geneva. He is in her class. Actually, I am sitting in between them. When I tell it at home that night I get a big laugh for sitting between Geneva and her boyfriend.

But I don't think he was her boyfriend. She doesn't have much of a social life on the farm. There is no way for her to have dates. She isn't going to have much chance to meet boys. And anyway Pop will probably run them off. At about this time Perry comes to Pop and says that he wants to marry Geneva. They must have a secret romance happening. Pop threatens to run him off the place if he hears anymore about it. Geneva isn't going to marry a farmhand.

In grade school and junior high the state provides you books, but you have to buy them in high school. There are other activity fees as well. Geneva always has to go to Pop and beg money for these things. He doesn't always give it to her. Finally, when she is a Junior, the year before I start school, she quits rather than endure the hassles. I think my older brothers and Geneva would all have done better in life if they could have completed high school.

She is a frail girl and after helping Mom with the cooking and ironing she likes to hide away in our living room that is always closed off. She lies on the couch and reads movie and romance magazines and dreams whatever young girls dream of in these days in the early forties. She makes grand chocolate fudge. I am a fool for her candy.

She goes away at the beginning of the war to work for a while in town. She comes back to live with us and one day a young soldier named Bill Land comes to visit. Geneva has met him while she lived in town. But now she is back living under Pop's roof and subject to all his rules. She is barely eighteen. The next morning we find a ladder under her window. Her soldier has come back in the night and spirited her away. Pop is fit to be tied and Perry, who still loves her, wants to go with Pop to town and see if they can catch them at the train or bus station. Pop decides to not do it.

Geneva writes that they have been married and a few months later they come back to the farm. Pop grudgingly shakes hands. He says that if Bill had not been a serviceman he would have run him off. A man should come and ask for a daughter's hand properly. But Geneva knows he never would have agreed. She has sized up the situation exactly right. Mom takes to Bill right off and hastens to town the next Saturday and buys a three-star decal to hang in the window. A star for Odell, one for Clyde, and one for her new son-in-law. She is closing in on Aunt Naomi who has four stars in her window for all of Uncle Lora's children.

Mom nearly has to take to her bed when Geneva writes her later in the war that she is divorcing Bill. We don't know it at the time, but she has met someone else. After she and Bill divorce she brings Sherman to meet us. She has written a letter to Pop and Mom, and she has made it clear to them if they don't accept Sherman, we won't be seeing her again. Sherman is a veteran and he and Pop hit it off. Later, Pop's opinion of him slips. Sherman is good-hearted, but he hasn't a lot of ambition and is never going to go far.

In the afternoon, the evenings stretch out into the bedtime hours. The long daylight hours allow me to walk about and see the city right up until bedtime. I explore everything. I wonder how long the soles on my shoes are going to last. I almost always wind up at the tennis courts watching the young men and women get in a set before going somewhere to a late dinner or on a late date. Although Juanita is coming to the city, she is not athletic so I know we will not be taking up tennis. I'm not sure how we will fill up our evenings. Take in a lot of shows probably. I have time to wonder where our relationship will take us.

We will probably go along in some fashion getting used to our new arrangement. We have said we will not count on the FBI job coming through, but that would be neat. I wonder if she could get me an application and get me hired on in Washington. What a great thing that would be. She said that FBI employees start off making $2,700 a year. That is not too great an amount, but it is nearly twice what I am making. And Washington is said to be an expensive town to live in. What could you get into to make real money? What jobs could I possibly fill? The FBI trains you for the work they want you to do. Most of it is in their fingerprint section. How would you ever learn how to classify fingerprints? I guess that if other people have learned to do it I could learn to do it. I hate to have to count on a job with them that might never happen. But what else am I able to do? I am never going to become a day laborer, or an assembly line worker. And farming is out of the question. I had been good at bookkeeping in high school. That was kind of what Forrest did in the personnel job. I still regret not getting that job even if I would have had to dodge the nefarious Bob Carroll. There are not going to be many well-paying jobs that I will be qualified for. Will I ever make good money? A thirty-five hundred dollar a year job is good money. Five thousand dollars is fabulous. Then you are getting up where doctors and lawyers walk. I regret not being able to go to college. A college education is what I really need to get ahead.

At night I lie in bed with the radio tuned low listening to the Colonels. The street is quiet and the house is quiet. The window is slightly open, and I can hear the breeze rustling the tree just outside my window. When a boarder comes in late, he moves quietly. Sometimes I hear him briefly in the bathroom. I am getting plenty of sleep and rest. When Juanita gets here I imagine we will be keeping late hours.

Chapter 4

I pull the bell cord, retrieve my suitcase from the overhead, and move up the aisle between the passengers. The driver looks up questioningly in the rear view mirror. There are no houses nearby. Why am I getting off out here in the middle of nowhere? I tell him, "at the top of the hill." Miller Station Road runs off to the right going back to our house about a mile down the road. It is a dangerous place to stop. People come up the road too fast and it is a hidden entrance. They tell of a fiery crash that happened here and burned a man to death. My sister and her husband were rear-ended here just a couple years ago, and she received neck injuries.

I alight quickly and wave the bus on. Carlisle is only a few miles farther. Then he will go on to Flemingsburg and Maysville. After that he will become the afternoon bus retracing his route back to Lexington. The suitcase is not heavy. I am bringing a change of underwear, and when I go back to Louisville tomorrow, I will use the little gym bag that I bought and carry inside the bigger suitcase to carry the couple things I need. From now on I won't have to carry the big suitcase around.

I am happy to be back and don't mind the walk in. During my last year of high school, I got off the school bus here every day and ran home to help Clyde with the crop. On the farm I ran everywhere, even though I had a bad heart. I liked to get around quick. It bothers me that in Louisville I have to walk everywhere. People would think I was odd, or maybe up to mischief, if they saw me running on the street. I am always impatient to get where I am going.

Everything along the road is familiar. We lived on a farm in Miller Station when Clyde and Odell came back from the army in 1945. We moved back to another farm here after Pop died. The place had been carved out from our earlier farm and the house on the place was the tenant house where Perry and Wynona had lived. Then we had moved down to another place that bordered on the train tracks that ran past our place and on in to Carlisle and down to Maysville. A single train came by each day. There was not much shipping by rail now and people thought we were going to lose the rail line. But it had been there in 1945 and I couldn't imagine the engine not going by every day.

I am in no hurry today and take pleasure in the greening of the farms along the road. It smells like things are growing. Tobacco fields are harrowed and worked to smooth them for planting the tobacco. The shoots for transplanting are pushing at the cotton coverings that protected them from frost in the past month. Corn is planted in the bottoms and has not yet pushed through the earth, but the alfalfa and clover are green and growing and will be ready for the first cutting later this spring. The cattle and sheep are enjoying the tender spring growth of grass and are swollen from eating the water-filled blades.

I remember how I used to wait and watch for kinfolks that were expected on Saturdays. Whether it was Geneva and Sherman coming in from Cincinnati, or Odell and Opal coming by on the way to her father's house, or Glen and Lillian stopping in for a while or maybe overnight, it was more than just a break in the routine. They brought an air of the big city. They had all lived on the farm like us and had escaped. They had seen new sights and new sounds. They had got away from the soul-grinding, body-fatiguing existence of the farm and had found something better.

I wonder if Clyde and Mom and Colleen now look forward to my return. I have gotten away like the others. But it somehow doesn't seem all that grand – all that satisfying. But it is a start

– just to get away. I won't be a mailboy in Louisville all my life. I feel it is just the first step to wherever I am going.

I top the hill by the tobacco barn and I see over in the field where Clyde is putting in his crop of tobacco. I have guilty feelings about not being here to help, but he will make out. I have another career. I am not going to talk much about it. It isn't a job I can brag on.

If the great depression had not come along, I would probably have grown up in a large town such as Covington or Latonia. We would have been across the river from my cousins who worked at the Fisher Body plant of Chevrolet in Cincinnati. We would have visited them on Sundays, and I would have played with my second cousins and enjoyed the companionship of all the kids in the neighborhood. I envy Clyde and Odell who have spent most of their childhoods in the environs of Covington.

Pop had first worked as the head of a section gang repairing track for the L & N railroad. That is when they moved to Latonia, just outside Covington. Then later he took a job with an oil refinery. But with the depression men were being laid off and wages cut. He moved our family back to the farm. Odell and Clyde were put to work by my father. They were new to the farm and farm ways. At first they floundered. They were shy of the animals and didn't know how to act around them. Pop laughingly tells of the time he put Odell to harrowing the tobacco field and he tried to turn too short. He found the horses nervously halted and the harrow tipped at an alarming angle about to overturn. These stories are amusing. Having been on the farm all my life, I am at ease around the animals and have driven a team from the time I could stand on a moving wagon.

Odell and Clyde work hard in the crops with little recompense. Pop is domineering and treats Clyde better than Odell. Odell is her oldest and Mom tries to take up for him. He is also the one most likely to get out from under Pop's dominance and starts seeing a girl in Lexington.

When Odell and Clyde turn 21 Pop gives each of them a party. He gives them watches. He gives Clyde a team of horses and Odell a used 1935 Plymouth. Each is well pleased with his gift. Pop throws them each a party. He invites aunts and uncles and cousins and other friends. We have a house full of people. Odell's party is in May when a lot of us can spill out of doors, but Clyde's is just after Christmas in cold weather. Betty Sue Hughes and Junior Jones and Uncle Lilburn's youngest children play with us. The young people of Odell and Clyde's ages try to have their own fun. Mary Gaunce seems to organize everything. I have never seen them at play. She gets them in a circle on their knees and they play spin the bottle. A lot of them are related, but are "kissing cousins." They pull Perry into the circle and Paul McCord and Uncle Lora's sons. Geneva is there too. When the bottle points to a brother or sister they spin again.

In the summer of 1941 both Odell and Clyde get drafted. We live far back off the Winchester Road. When Clyde has to report, a dispatch rider comes across our hill on a motorcycle to tell him where to come the next morning and the time to be there. Of course, we aren't yet at war, but things are ominous and Mom is worried about her boys. Before Odell leaves, he marries the girl he has been seeing. Pop marks it as a foolish act. Odell has to send her an allotment check. Clyde sends his money to Pop who puts it in the bank for him.

Pop is right because she spends the money and divorces Odell as soon as he gets back from the South Pacific. Clyde saves enough money during the war to buy a farm and he puts a tenant on it. During the war Mom worries about my brothers and writes them frequently. She reads their letters home to us kids. By the end of the war I am old enough that I have written some letters of my own to the two of them. There are some happy days in 1945 when each of them returns to us safely.

I pull the old Dodge off the road and into the weeds at the entrance to the barn off Concord Road. Juanita and I want to talk a while. I had picked her up earlier and she had gone to Paris with us. We didn't really want to go to a movie, but we had nowhere else to go. So after we all got back to our house I had brought her on home to Oxbow Hill. But we want to talk a while first.

"So where exactly is the room you rented?" I ask.

"It's on a street called Floral Court. It runs between Sixth and Seventh Streets and is only a block or two from Ormsby."

She had her sister, Ruth, take her to Louisville one day after I had written and told her about getting my room, and she had tried to locate as near to me as possible.

"Then at morning you can ride the Sixth or Fourth Street buses downtown and walk on over to your work." She was going to work for a stationery company that made up wedding invitations, birth announcements, and other special cards and boxed them and shipped them out. She was going to be working right downtown. I went in the other direction at morning.

"And sometimes if there is a good movie playing downtown or we want to meet for dinner, I'll just stay there and you can catch a bus and meet me somewhere."

"Okay, but with the overtime I have to work every day, you'll be off at least an hour ahead of me."

"That's all right. I can do some shopping while I wait."

"We had better try to save our money. Did you hear anything from the FBI?" She had talked to an agent that visited her school. She had filled out an application. If she got a job, it would probably be in Washington. We had decided not to talk much about it. And if she were contacted, we would decide then if she wanted to go or not.

"Not yet. But one of the neighbors and one of the teachers told me they had talked to an agent that contacted them about me."

"I'm surprised that more of your class didn't fill out applications. They didn't come around last year or I probably would have."

"Oh, you wouldn't have left me," she says smugly and nestles deeper into my arms.

"I guess not, but it would be nice if somehow I could have gone ahead and they could have investigated you and been ready to offer you the job as soon as you graduated."

"Don't talk about it. It probably won't happen. Ruby and Patsy filled out applications, but they probably won't go."

"It's hard to leave your home."

"I don't know why people can't get away from Nicholas County. It's like they are rooted to the ground. They are like trees that grow and are ready to bloom. Then instead they just die and rot where they are."

I'd heard that before. It was what she said to me when she was trying to get me to leave.

"Anyway, you say you like your job?" She brings her attention back to me.

"I said I like the people. A monkey could do my job."

"Well maybe when I get down there, we can find something else for you."

The moon is swimming through the trees. It is a warm night. I think of the nights during the winter that we had parked here and the piercing cold we had endured. I warmly anticipate the summer coming up in Louisville away from the scrutiny of her foster parents. Where we can explore and enjoy the city. There will be no curfews or rules. We will have money to do whatever we want. A new life awaits us.

No one tells me when the war starts. It's too bad. I am in the second grade and I would have remembered the moment and the circumstances. Maybe I am told but it isn't much of a jolt. Clyde and

Odell are already gone and Pearl Harbor is far away. The Hawaiian Islands are something you see in a Maria Montez movie.

It seems like the war affects everybody. Some of the kids at school have fathers in the service. My own father seems ancient. I can't imagine a father being that young. Few of them have older brothers in as we do. But they have cousins or uncles serving and so do we. People with family members serving hang or paste stars in their windows. If a family member is killed in the war, the star changes to gold.

My father blames the president for getting us involved. He has voted for FDR in 1940 when he runs on a platform of avoiding the European war. Pop feels betrayed and Mom echoes his sentiments. Now they have two sons in danger. My parents never have a good word to say about FDR and it colors my opinion of him.

Aunt Naomi and Uncle Lora's sons go into service. Cee is drafted into the navy. Aunt Mary Liz's son, Paul, is in the marines. We are an army family. I have never known anyone in those other branches of service before. Clyde writes home that they want him to transfer to the Army Air Force. He is small and they want to make him a tail gunner. It is Mom's job to correspond with the boys, but Pop takes up a pencil on this occasion and writes Clyde back telling him to stay where he is. According to Pop, when you are in a plane, they can shoot at you and kill you or they can shoot the plane down and you can be killed in the crash. The same for the navy. They can shoot you, or the ship can go down and you drown. Better to stay in the infantry where you can only be shot. It improves your chances by half he argues.

Aside from having my brothers away, the war mainly affects me by the shortages it causes. Sugar is rationed and Mom no longer makes as many pies and cakes. She saves the sugar rationing stamps to have sugar on hand for canning preserves. Pop buys an old truck so he can get extra rationing stamps for gasoline. He applies for extra allowances because of being a farmer. We have plenty of gasoline compared to other folks. A lot of my favorite candy disappears from the store shelves. It is going to the soldiers, and I stifle my complaints. But I sorely miss

Hershey bars and other forms of chocolate. The deprivation hones a sweet tooth that I am unable to satisfy for years.

Other shortages affect us. The school participates in scrap drives. There is a lot of old scrap metal lying about the farm and we are usually able to add something to the pile. Bond drives come one after the other and we take dimes to school and buy war stamps and paste them in our books. We sing the popular war songs like "Praise the Lord and Pass the Ammunition" and "Coming in on a Wing and a Prayer." And the sentimental ones like "White Cliffs of Dover" and "When the Lights Come on Again all Over the World." If you ask me what I remember most about my childhood, it is the war.

I carry Juanita's suitcases onto the city bus. She has brought two suitcases, each one larger than the one I brought down two weeks ago. She must have more than just clothing packed into them. They weigh a ton. It is my first experience in moving all the personal belongings of a woman. It is late Sunday afternoon, and there are few people on the bus, so we can sit near the front and don't have to worry about blocking the aisle with the suitcases.

Juanita has been spared the worry I had about finding a place to stay. She is looking forward to getting settled. We ride the Fourth Street bus out because this is the same bus she will have to ride downtown tomorrow to her new job. The bus system is handy, although you sometimes have to wait for upwards of an hour to get the next one. A car might be nice to have, but we aren't going to miss it too much.

We alight at the edge of Central Park and walk across. Floral Court is just on the other side. I walk down past here every morning. I will notice it but will be leaving earlier than she, so there is scant chance we'll see each other at morning.

The elderly lady she is staying with, Mrs. Keegan, eyes me doubtfully. She is a widow, and she rents the extra bedroom on her first floor and a second floor apartment out for income. Juanita can sit in her living room, but will have to eat her meals out, same as me. Mrs. Keegan keeps her shades drawn and the house dark. It is cool but has a musk about it like old mold and lavender. Juanita's bedroom is just off the living room and can be separated by sliding doors. The bed is big with a deep mattress. The room is much smaller than mine, but I don't have the run of the house.

She drops her suitcases, and we go off to get some supper. I take her over to the drug store on Oak Street. We talk about our plans for the week. We agree that we will usually just meet somewhere in the evening. I don't want to seem to be a pest to Mrs. Keegan. She has promised Ruth to look after Juanita. We don't know to what extent she will keep her charge.

Juanita wants to get back to unpack. We walk along the edge of the park. We stop to sit for a while on one of the benches and watch the tennis players in their pretty white shorts and skirts. It all feels different. Not at all like when we were going together in Nicholas County. We are here in Louisville among a different sort of people now. Here people play tennis and stroll in the park. Here they go to the metropolitan center of town and see shows and have a choice of restaurants. There is a zoo and an amusement park and if you go down to the waterfront you can watch barges and large boats go by and occasionally an ornate riverboat. It is a place from another world, and it has been here all along barely 80 miles from the ragged county where we have lived.

*   *   *

Emmaline Longbottom Roe and Filmore
Roe with Granddaughters Gladys Hughes,
Emma Roe, and Cleophus Roe, early 1920's

*   *   *

Chapter 5

My whole life I have not liked my name of Lynwood. When I come to work at Jones-Dabney people ask me what I want to be called. It had not occurred to me before that you could choose your name. My first name is Charles, but Mom never wanted me to go by that. She surmised correctly that people would corrupt it to Charlie. I didn't feel like a Charlie. I had never been called that. What galled me most were that relatives continued to call me Snookie even after I started to school and everyone there called me Lynwood. Jimmy had nicknamed me Snookie after our cat which had got its name from the comic strips. In the thirties and forties a lot of people named their pets after Smoky Stover's cat, Snookie, who was always walking around with a bandage on its tail.

So I am presented with an opportunity to choose a new name. But I don't want to always be explaining it. I tell everyone that I go by Lynwood, but that everyone calls me "Woodie" for short. And Woodie it is. That seems right for a mailboy. A new name feels right for the new life I am leading. Juanita chuckles about it, but goes right on calling me Lynwood.

As we move into summer, I shed my jacket and get some sensible clothing. There is no need to wear good dress pants around the plant. You are liable to brush against some paint or creosote and ruin them. On the farm I wore a set of pants and shirt for a week and changed to a clean set on Sunday. With my first pay I buy two pairs of jeans. I have brought long sleeved shirts with me and go back to wearing jeans for a week at a time and alternating two shirts. I take my clothes to a laundry that is only a short way from the post office. They are very hard on material, but the clothing comes back clean and pressed and my little bit is only pennies for the week. During the summer they only misplace one sock and when I call in a panic, they are able to find it from my minute description. With my money situation the purchase of a new pair of socks has to be evaluated against other needs.

Pauline leaves the switchboard to be replaced by Aggie's daughter, Bev. Bev is about twenty and newly married. She and her new husband have moved in with Aggie. Aggie dotes on them, but it sounds as though the new marriage is not going all that smoothly. Bev likes to stay up at night and can't get going at morning. So although Aggie and Pauline have rotated the shifts, Aggie begins coming in early every morning and Bev stays late in the afternoons. Bev is nearer to my age and we talk easily. She is an attractive girl but not beautiful. Sometimes when Bev is delayed in coming in for one reason or the other, Pauline comes by and fills in to take some of the calls when the board is swamped.

I see Pauline on all my mail runs. She has moved up to the Accounting Section at the back of the second floor. About fifteen women work in there. They are always terribly busy. They always seem harried as if they do not have time to accomplish all the tasks that are given them. A large statuesque woman, Pamela Brown, is over them and keeps them hopping. When I say large woman, she is just that. She is well over six feet tall. She belongs to some social club where the women are over six feet and the men something like six four or more. It is so they can date people more near their own stature. I have never given any thought to oversize people having this problem. The club seems like a good solution to their problem. Pamela is always talking about some fellow she is going out with that she has first met at one of the club's get-togethers.

We always have colored workers on the farm. There is a black community nearby and word gets around over there that we need hands at tobacco planting and housing and stripping times. They come over as day hands, sometimes four or five to a car. We seldom feed them, but when we have to, Mom makes them wait and eat at a second table. There is never any trouble about them. I guess they have gotten used to the prejudices they face. Of course, all the white work hands refer to them as "niggers" and Pop is afraid that we kids will say it to their faces sometimes. He solemnly tells us that we are not to do this within their hearing. When we are around them we are to call them "darkies." Even we know better than to do this. He is from another century.

During the war we more often get colored help as most of the white men go to the war. Of course, some of the blacks go, too. But not so many. Mom says it is because they have flat feet and can't march. We believe her. We pick up a lot of misinformation from Mom.

A colored man, Charlie Davis, comes to stay and brings his family – his wife and two little girls, the oldest my age. Pop and Perry fix up one of the stalls in the racehorse barn, and they live there. We play with the girls. The oldest one has something wrong with her tongue and drools all the time. One day we are wrestling and she gets me down and hangs over me and slobbers in my face. I throw her off and won't play with her any more.

Another colored man named Emmet also works by the month and stays in the barn. But he eats his meals with us. Rather than wait at a second table Mom sets him a plate at a side utility table so he can eat at the same time and we pass the food to the side table. So he eats with us but not with us. Mom and Pop have strange ideas of probity. When Colleen gets Scarlet Fever we are quarantined by the county health nurse and can't go out for a while. Everyone in the family has to have their throats swabbed, Perry included. Emmet laughs at him and Pop who are dreading the ordeal. While she is swabbing all of us, and we see that it isn't too bad an experience, Pop asks the nurse if she can't swab Emmet. She says it isn't necessary, but Pop explains to her that he wants her to do it as a joke. Perry gleefully goes and brings Emmet to the house. He is crestfallen and enters hat in hand and endures the trial. Pop and Perry give him the ho-ho in the days that follow.

The black community isn't far away if you cut through the fields. We have a smart shepherd dog named "Tip" that we got before the war, and Clyde and O'Dell have taught him to round up the cows and drive them to the barn at milking time. He disappears and later Perry says he found out that one of the black work hands has admired him and has slipped over to our house while we were at town and took Tip. Pop doesn't want trouble so they don't go get Tip back. I am sorry to lose Tip. It lowers black people in my estimation.

One of the jobs of the accounting section is to make up the payroll. Everybody is paid in cash. It is sealed in envelopes and handed out by your boss on payday. Mr. Gerlach or Madelaine always give me my pay. The black workers that toil over in the paint shed pushing the big barrels and stacking the cartons of gallon buckets are paid every Friday. I carry a big envelope that contains their individual pay envelopes over to them on Friday afternoon. I soon find out that they watch for it and won't tolerate it being even a few minutes late. The paint shed is at the end of my mail run, but I discover that it is better to alter my route when I am carrying the pay and take it by and give it to their boss before making my run.

"Yessir. My, my, that old bird is flying this way," I hear them say as I approach.

"That eagle fly this way, shore nuff."

"I hear him. He gonna drop a big load. Gonna drop it right on us."

Everybody is enjoying it tremendously. Their hard work is going to be rewarded. The eagle is flying. I hand the envelope off to the foreman.

"Yes, yes. My lord, he jes' dropped it."

"Shit all over us. Fine bird it is. Big load of shit."

I get into the spirit. As I walk away I fold my hands under my armpits like Red Skelton and flap my arms and make a "smock, smock" call. They are delighted. They call after me.

"We'll be watching. Watching for that eagle to fly back over thisaway."

After that I have to make my flapping gesture and "smock, smock" call every time I bring over the pay envelopes. On my usual rounds, they make banter about the eagle not dropping his load this time around.

The paint-shed workers have lives like the white workers outside Jones-Dabney. Blacks are only employed in the paint shed. Their foreman is white. It is 1953. It all seems okay to me. Segregation of the races is just beginning to crack a little, but it has not come to Louisville. In a few years the town will be embroiled in bitter civil rights marches. But everything is calm this year.

One of the workers is in some trouble with the court. His wife is divorcing him, and he has to pay her alimony. He neglects to do this, and she gets her lawyer to get a judgment against him and has his wages garnished. The lawyer can't get his address so he uses Jones-Dabney for his corresponding address. One of the letters comes in and it appears to be something for one of the salesmen. I open it to see where it should go. It relates to the legal matter and Mr. Gerlach is furious that I have looked at it. The man complains and I have to apologize to him. Personnel gets involved, too, and I apologize again. I wonder if they are going to have to fire me before it quiets down. But eventually it all blows over. I get some dirty looks as I drop the mail off at the paint shed. Dirty looks everyday except on payday.

As we approach Clay City we can see the big mountains looming ahead to the east. The country is lush and green now into June. Pop is using up some of his precious rationed gas to go see Sonny Martin. We need help in the tobacco crop. Sonny had come to us a couple years ago and brought his oldest boys still at home. He has a bevy of children — fourteen in all — ranging in age from pre-school up to mid-twenties. The oldest boy has joined the army back in the thirties and is now a Master Sergeant.

Up a hollow we find the Martin homeplace. It is rough country and maybe that is why a colored family can afford such a big farm. Mrs. Martin and one of the girls, who looks to be pregnant, are at the house. She tells us Sonny and the others are off picking blackberries. She says we can drive on down a dirt road and find them. It looks like we are getting deeper and deeper into the wilderness. We are driving on roads that Pop shouldn't try with our new Pontiac.

We find them and Pop and Sonny shake hands like old friends. Sonny says the kids will all be coming along in a few minutes and he expects they have enough blackberries by now and we can go along to the house. They start coming out of the briars and you never saw the like of Martins. He sadly tells us that one of the boys he had sent to us last year is now in the army and another is working elsewhere. If he had known Pop was needing help, he would have sent him to us. He tells us to drive back to the house and he will think it over and maybe he can still help. The children are standing about gazing at the shiny maroon Pontiac. Sonny says that two of the children have never ridden in a car. Pop doesn't wait to be asked but loads them right in to give them their first ride. Jimmy and I get in the front seat and look back at them sitting like stones afraid to touch anything.

Sonny has one of the big boys bring out a bucket of cold water and gives us drinks. I'm not happy to be drinking with colored folks, but Pop likes these particular people, and I am thirsty. Water from their bucket tastes the same as ours. Sonny says he was thinking about our problem on the way back, and he thinks he can send his two oldest remaining boys with us. Starr is sixteen and Noble is fourteen. Pop is doubtful, but Sonny vouches for them. If they don't give a good day's work, Pop is to tell him and he will make it satisfactory. I don't know what he means. Is he going to give Pop the wages back? More likely he is going to beat the tar out of them. He sends them to get their clothes together while he and Pop talk some more.

On the way back to the Bluegrass, Starr and Noble are wide-eyed and interested in the countryside. They haven't got out much I suppose. They are practically non-communicative, but they whisper back and forth. I get to like them a lot. They also sleep in the racehorse barn, but they take their meals with us. Mom doesn't like cooking for them, and she complains that she has accidentally left the cherry preserves on the table one evening – these are the cherries that Clyde has knocked out of the tree with his big cane fishing pole the year he went into the army – and before she can recover them from the table, Noble has rolled half the jar out onto his plate.

When they come to us, neither of them has shoes. Pop says they can't work in the fields and in the stubble of the hay fields barefoot. He takes them to town and buys them work shoes. He uses ration stamps from our books to get them. Mom has a fit about it. She says we need the stamps ourselves. Is he going to let his own children go barefoot?

Starr and Noble are with us all that summer and are good workers. After supper, they sit on the porch and listen to our radio through the window. When Mom and Pop aren't around, they get us kids to wind up the Victrola that Geneva has given the family and play records for them. We have a recording of "Don't Get Around Much Anymore" that they are crazy about.

Over in the R & D building, one of the laboratories is run by a man named Walter Abell. His son works in the R & D building in another laboratory. He is the sometimes boyfriend of Virginia Gray, the girl in the front office. But Walter is not anybody's boyfriend. He is a disagreeable sort, really. I run afoul of him on some paint order. These orders come in to one of the offices in the main office building and they type up the specifications and send them over to R & D. They concoct the right ingredients and might mix up a little batch to see that it is what the customer wants. Then they order the materials, if they don't already have them on hand, and turn it over to the people back in the mixing shed to produce the quantity the customer wants and ship it to him.

Walter has been tipped off by someone that an order is coming over to his laboratory and to expect it. He is waiting for me. I have no paint order. He makes me search through all the mail. On my next run the same thing happens. He comes to the office where I sort the mail and looks all around and behind the table where I work. He grumbles and goes off to check with the office that was supposed to send the order to him. I don't know why they just don't type up a new order. Apparently the key information is on the sheet he thinks I have misplaced.

The next day we go through the same routine. He gets Mr. Gerlach involved. He thinks I have lost or misplaced the order. He thinks I have been careless or worse. I can't explain it. He won't believe that I have not seen his order. Of all the people in the chain who have handled it, he focuses on me as the one most likely to have lost it.

They must resolve it some way. Probably they simply called the customer and had him send them another order or read his requirements over the telephone. I can't avoid Walter. I have to deliver mail to his laboratory four times a day. Periodically, he still gets up from his desk and takes the mailbag from me and looks through it for the lost order.

On the lower part of the tobacco patch Pop leaves several large plants standing when the rest of the crop is housed. These are the best plants that he has grown, and he is careful to keep worms off these plants so that the leaves are smooth and perfect. He does not top them with the rest of the crop and the blooms are allowed to fully mature and then he cuts them carefully and hangs them in the smokehouse to dry. He leaves the topped plants in the field a while longer, but the leaves do not spread much beyond what they have at the time of the topping because the plants have already stopped growing.

When the blooms have dried out they are crushed and the seeds taken for next year's crop. This is a precautionary measure in case seeds are not otherwise obtainable. But each year he goes to the Experiment Station and buys new seeds that are supposed to yield plants that are resistant to various types of crop diseases. These we put out in 100-foot tobacco beds in the spring. The beds are carefully plowed and burned over to kill the weeds, fertilized, and covered with canvas to protect against frost and stray animals that will ordinarily not walk out onto the white canvas.

So the seeds he takes from the blooms of the most recent crop are a hedge against something happening so that he cannot obtain new seeds. He occasionally adds some of the seeds he has harvested to the other seeds if the past year's crop has been a particularly good one. He never keeps the seeds beyond the next year.

The stalks of tobacco that have produced the seeds are cut and hung separately from the rest of the crop. Most of them do not go to market. When the leaves have partially dried, they are stripped away, opened, and laid on bales of hay to finish drying.

Then one weekend Glenn and Lillian and the girls come to visit us. They have stopped by Uncle Joe's house and brought him and Aunt Matt with them. On Friday night Pop brings the best leafs of the tobacco he has set aside to the shed near the house and sprays them to dampen them and covers them with burlap sacks. He has chosen only the best leaves – the bright leaves – of the burley.

The next morning Pop brings the tobacco leaves into the house. He puts them in the floor in the middle of the room. Pop, Perry, Glenn, and Uncle Joe pull in straight-backed chairs from the kitchen and sit in a circle around the tobacco. Perry takes a cutting board and takes each leaf and carefully cuts the tough center stem out with his pocketknife. This leaves the leaf in two parts and he carefully places them together and makes a pile of them. The others take several of the leaf parts and *hold them in their hands and twist them into plugs. There is a special technique to it and Pop and Uncle Joe laugh at Glenn and Perry's first attempts to master it.*

When properly made the plugs are small and dark and tightly wound. Good plugs are dropped into a burlap sack. Sometimes the act of twisting the tobacco results in a fractured plug and this is put into another pile. Uncle Joe will crumble it up later and either chew it or stuff it into his pipe. Uncle Joe has a curved pipe like Sherlock Holmes favored, and he fills it with burley that is not aromatic like store-bought pipe tobacco, but is stout enough to make your head swim.

Pop does not ordinarily chew, but he stuffs some into his jaw to be sociable. He has chewed when he worked on the railroad and in the refinery where smoking was not permitted. Glenn and his brother, Homer, work in Cincinnati at the auto plant and are allowed to smoke only during breaks. So they chew at other times. Uncle Joe mostly smokes his pipe and Aunt Matt, a highly religious woman, tolerates it. But she constantly berates the filthy habit and the odors he is causing in the house.

When they finish twisting the tobacco, they have two burlap sacks full of plugs. Pop keeps one and hangs it in the smokehouse. He gives the other one to Glenn who promises to give part of the bag to Homer. As far as I know neither Pop nor Perry ever use any of the plugs we keep. Later, Glenn visits again and Pop gets the sack out and gives him most of the other plugs. Pop and Perry are both addicted to cigarettes. They smoke constantly in the field, in the barns, and in the house. Luckily, the old farmhouse has high ceilings and most of the smoke rises over our heads to the far recesses of the rooms.

One other small incident mars my time as the Jones-Dabney mail clerk. We have an antique metering machine. Periodically, I have to take the meter to the post office and have postage added to it. It is a big steel monstrosity, and you have to put a little water in a reservoir from time to time. You can slide an unsealed envelope through a slot and it will wet and seal it and stamp the correct postage on it. In theory that's what it should do. About one time in five it malfunctions and jams and crumples the letter. If I have only a few letters, I lick them myself and stick them in the slot to trip the postage stamper.

But sometimes they bring me in dozens of letters to go out and if the meter is feeling okay, these can be done in a short time. For the few that crumple, I get some spare envelopes and smooth out the insert and put it in a new envelope. Three or four times I am given a massive mailing to get out late in the afternoon. These are probably advertising letters to go out to all our customers or something. Anyhow, they all need postage, and I have to work like the devil to make the six o'clock mailing. When I can't get through in time, I stop where I am and mail what I have ready. The others don't get out that night, but I put them in the mailbox anyway after I finish.

When I have these massive mailings, I have a ton of crumpled envelopes. I have been told to save these as the office will be reimbursed for the unused postage on them. I stuff them in a big envelope in the table. When it is about full the first time after I start to work, I take the scissors and carefully cut around the postage. They don't need the entire envelope to see that the postage is not cancelled. When I get to the post office, there is a big flap. They have some rule that they have to have the entire envelope. They call Mr. Gerlach. They have a long talk and eventually I am credited with the unused postage on the meter that I have brought in to be adjusted. When I get back to the office I am chewed out for cutting up the envelopes. It's another case of nobody telling me the right way to do it. I am chastised. I don't like to mess up. I feel like a dope when these things are called to my attention. Like I grew up dumb and uninformed on the farm.

Chapter 6

We leave Juanita's house on Floral Court and walk along the north side of Central Park and wait on the Fourth Street bus that will take us to Iroquois Park. Iroquois Park is a huge wilderness of greenery on the southern outskirts of Louisville. It has a large hill and several overlooks where you can view the town. But the overlooks are far from the park entrance. You need a car to drive up to them. Maybe someday we will have a car and drive to the overlooks and drive all around Louisville.

The bus route follows Fourth Street for a while. Then cuts over to Third and goes past Churchill Downs where we can see the grandstand with its twin spires but cannot see any of the track hidden behind the wall. We go on down past Standiford Field where we sometimes spot a passenger plane landing or taking off with people bound for distant places. Airline travel is still in its infancy and traveling by plane is not only an adventure, but felt to be somewhat dangerous also. Crashes and midair collisions are reported at length by the media. The loss of life is always tremendous. It is akin to the stories at the turn of the century about great train disasters. But they don't write songs about plane crashes. We think that some evening we will just ride down to Standiford Field and watch the planes land and take off.

The last part of the bus's route is along Taylor Boulevard. Beautiful houses line both sides of Taylor, and we point out our favorites and talk about what it must be like to live in those big new houses. We have both left old farm houses. The places where I have lived were always old but usually big because of the size of our family and all the furniture we had. Juanita's family has lived in smaller houses. The place where they live now is only five rooms. We see a particularly grand place and promise ourselves that someday we will come back and buy it.

Taylor Boulevard ends at the entrance to Iroquois park. Juanita has borrowed a blanket from Mrs. Keegan for us to sit on. She told her we were going on a picnic but we have not brought any food. We walk up into the park to where the stage is built. It is an outdoor stage, and they hold outdoor performances in the summer. Seats are set in rows facing the stage, and several performers are rehearsing a festival of dance. We spread the blanket outside the fence beside the walk and watch the activity onstage. A young woman is called on and the "Theme from Ruby Gentry" plays over the speakers. She moves into a slow, languorous interpretive dance. She makes eye contact with us and dances for us. She is lovely. She finishes. We want to clap, but we are not supposed to be there. She walks to the back of the stage and joins the other dancers. She looks back at us. I raise my hands and mime silent applause.

Dusk is falling and we fold up our old blanket and walk a little farther into the park. It is Friday night and we do not have to be at work on the morrow. It is a luxury I never had on the farm where chores had to be done all mornings. We can stay up late, but we are creatures of habit. Years of early bedtimes remain rooted in us. We loll on the blanket listening to the songs being played at the stage. We talk and kiss with none of the urgency that marked our earlier courtship. We have all the time in the world.

We live four miles from the Lexington city line on the Winchester Road. The road is mostly lined with stately old horse farms. We live so far back off the road that Pop or Perry usually takes us by car out to the road to wait for the school bus at mornings. Anna Katherine, who lives at the top of the hill and is in the eighth grade, catches a ride with us most mornings.

While we are waiting, Pop tunes the radio to the early morning music coming from Renfro Valley on WHAS, the Louisville station. Pop mostly listens to WHAS and WLW in Cincinnati. We listen to the fiddlers and guitar players and hear the talk about how cold it is in Renfro Valley this morning and what is happening on their farms. It is all real folksy.

We are among the first children that are picked up by the school bus that travels the roads near town. The bus turns at Bryant Road nearby and goes back toward town. We pass through Cadentown and travel along Liberty Road. The kids farther out in the country go to rural schools. We go to Kenwick on Henry Clay Boulevard. It is a beautiful building with marble floors. It is an elementary school and each grade is split among three homerooms. When you reach seventh grade, you go to Bryan Station Junior High and then on to Lafayette High School. The kids in the city will attend Henry Clay High School.

We have to be at the bus stop early at mornings. The buses are used to run a second route to pick up some of the city kids who live far from the school. Kenwick gets a lot of kids from the country and most of those from the east side of Lexington. The next school over is Maxwell school. That is where the kids went before Kenwick was built. Some of the kids live near the line between the two schools. They try to attend Kenwick if they can. We think we have a great school. One of the teachers pens a school song and we all meet in the gym and sing it.

> Dear little Kenwick, best school in the land,
> Here's to the boys and girls, they're a royal band.
> When school days are over, in this world we'll roam,
> We'll always think of Kenwick as our dearest home school home.

On the first day of school Mom and Geneva get me ready. I have a new lunch box. They say to tell my teacher that my name is Lynwood. I have never heard it before. I've always been called Snookie. They scratch my name on my lunch box, but when I get to school I have forgotten it. I can't tell anyone my name. Mrs. Forsyth will not let us go to lunch until I tell her. I have forgotten that it is on my lunch box. She sends to Jimmy's room to ask him my name, but he has forgotten also. She sends a note home to have my mother write my name down for her. My mother is mortified.

I recover from the inauspicious start. I am assigned locker number 1 to share with Delbert Pickett. Two years earlier my brother, Jimmy, and Delbert's brother, Gordon, have had the same locker. I think I am a favorite of Mrs. Forsyth. She is a kindly patient old gray-haired lady. Her daughter teaches the second grade, and I am bound for her the next year.

Since we have to wait for the late bus to take us home, we sometimes help the janitor collect the trash in the afternoon, and he gives us each a dime a week. We take the trash out and dump it in a wire enclosure where the janitor will burn it later. Sometimes the town kids on their way home stop to see what we are doing. A nerdy kid in an expensive coat stops and talks to us. He is my age. He is from a wealthy family. Nobody likes him much. But I hear more of John Y. Brown, Jr. in later years.

Throughout my school years I never dated. I never had as much as a mild flirtation at school. On some of the class trips I tried to sit with girls on the school bus, but they mostly ignored me. I liked girls – a lot. But none of them would give me a tumble. They went for the basketball players, and other rotters. The boys who dated talked about their dates and what they had done. They were scornful of the girls for the most part and ran down their reputations. I had a poor opinion of girls. They chased after the dumbest, foulest-mouthed boys in the class who treated them like dirt. Here I was a nice guy who would never treat them like that.

But I graduated and it looked like I was bound for bachelorhood and a life on the farm. Then, on the last weekend, Billy Doyle came to me and asked why I didn't give Juanita Caswell a chance. The girl was crazy about me, he said. I was the original guy without a clue. I talked with her. I couldn't drive so I had no way to date her now that school was over. I found that she came to Paris on Saturday with her Aunt and Uncle and often attended the movie. That was hard to believe. I'd been coming every Saturday for eleven years, and I had never seen her there.

My buddy, Doug, drove and we had been planning to attend a weenie roast that the Juniors were throwing for the graduating Seniors at Blue Licks Park. I asked Juanita. She said she would go with me. We had to get a date for Doug. Her best friend, Wilma Jo, who was the sister of my own sister-in-law, was liked by Doug. We tried to get her to come, but she said her father would not allow her to date. We drove out to the farm and talked to them and convinced them to let her come with us. We promised to be home early.

Juanita and Wilma Jo met us at the park. We could only talk with the others around, but there would be the drive back to her place when we would get better acquainted. I ate a hotdog and drank a Coke. My classmates could not believe that I was there with Juanita Caswell. Well, they had all missed their chances.

We left early in Doug's old car. Though Doug was enamored of her, Wilma Jo was not overly fond of Doug. She had come along as a favor to Juanita. She sat in the front seat beside Doug but didn't cuddle against him as a real sweetheart would have done. I wasn't sure how to act. Dating was a new adventure for me. Juanita and I sat close in the backseat and held hands. I had one shock when she said, "You don't do much work do you?" I thought she was chiding me on my lack of forwardness, but she explained that my hands were soft, lacking calluses, and that she thereby deduced that I did little manual labor. She was wrong, but at that time of year we were just getting ready to set out the tobacco. We weren't into the heavy work.

I had planned to kiss her before we got to her house, but I was shocked to learn that her cousin was picking her up in Carlisle, and we had almost arrived. Wilma Jo was also going to go back with them. So I let my chance go by. Doug too, had nothing to show for his gas spent and automobile use but a thank you. I let Juanita go reluctantly. She promised we would meet at the show on Saturday. I would have the opportunity then to realize my first kiss. In reality it took several weeks to work up the courage to kiss her in the back rows of the Paris theater.

On the school bus I see the older kids passing around a Mighty Mouse comic book. I want to look at it, too, but they won't let me have it. When we go to town on Saturday, Jim goes off to the movie. I follow Mom around. We are in the ten-cent store. I ask her to buy me a comic book. She agrees and asks which one I want. I am unfamiliar with comic books, and I don't know who Mighty Mouse is. I try to describe him. The lady says they don't have any about a mouse but how about a rabbit? I agree and that is how I came to own my first Bugs Bunny comic book.

After that Jim and I buy a comic book or two nearly every Saturday after coming out of the movie. We never miss a Looney Tunes and Merry Melodies or Walt Disney comic. Pop likes to read them, too. Pop won't let us buy adventure or detective comic books or those about super heroes. But later we trade our old comics for some of those. I like Captain Marvel better than Superman. I like Spy Smasher best of all. I dress up in my aviator's cap with a tea towel for a cape and ride my scooter pretending that I am Spy Smasher on the trail of Nazi agents. I am thrilled when they make a movie serial of him.

Comic books are a big commodity for trading. We arrange for someone else at school to bring their comics, and we meet at recess or, even better, on the school bus, and look over their goods and they look at ours. We cull out comics we already have or have seen. We usually trade straight up, but sometimes two good new ones are traded for three ragged ones. We have to keep comics hidden from the teachers who will confiscate them. Several of the boys would not have learned to read if it were not for comic books.

Comics are a favorite gift to give your friends at Christmas. They are only a dime, and you can roll them up and wrap them and tuck the edges of the paper back inside the bookends. On the farm, if we are not in the field, we are usually tucked in beside the big battery-powered radio reading comics. Jim and I devour them. Colleen had rather be playing with her paper doll cutouts.

By the time I am out of grade school, I have discovered pulp magazines which are only fifteen or twenty cents. Clyde buys science fiction magazines – Amazing Stories *and* Fantastic Tales. *Sometimes he gets* Stories of Adventure. *It takes a week to get through all the stories in the books. I like sports and there are even pulp magazines that are full of fiction about them written by Roe Richmond and George Lewis. I think it would be fun to write stories for these magazines. I think I will try when I get older.*

By the time I am in high school, I have pretty much graduated from comic books and pulp magazines to library books. I explore the shelves at Nicholas County High School. I read everything that looks promising. We buy books from a book club at school. We have boxes of comic books, big little books, and pulp magazines stored away upstairs. On one of our last moves from one farm to another, we decide to get rid of a lot of old stuff including these boxes of books that no one reads any more. Geneva doesn't want her boys to have them. We load them onto a wagon and take them back to the hollow and throw them into a sinkhole to stop its eroding.

Mrs. Keegan is an elderly widow. She has little income which she supplements by renting out her second floor as an apartment and the extra bedroom she has on the first floor. Juanita has been up to the apartment which a young married couple rents and she describes it as a little "doll house." She wishes we could live in it. Mrs. Keegan is a very respectable lady and an avid churchgoer. She is the member of a Catholic Church. The first I have known. She goes to church often during the week and goes early on Sunday. She is so constant in her attendance that I go around to see Juanita after she has left. She would be scandalized if she knew we were meeting like this. It is hard for us to find private places to be together. We watch the clock and I depart well before she returns from church.

Floral Court is only a block from my place on Ormsby. Juanita's family does not know we live so close to each other, but they know that we will continue our courting in Louisville. I'm not sure they approve of me. Her cousin who lives with them takes every chance to run me down. He says that Juanita was engaged to a boy who is in Korea. She took his ring, so he said. Juanita says it was a friendship ring and that she is no longer interested in him if she ever was. She says her cousin wants her for himself and he is jealous of any boy she gets serious about.

Juanita has dated several other boys. I have dated no one else. I am jealous of her other boy friends too. But this summer – here in Louisville – there is no one else. We are alone. We spend all the time we want together. We explore downtown. We explore our own neighborhood. There is no one to set a curfew on us. There is no one to watch us closely or critically. We set our own rules. We both must be up early on workdays. After work we meet at various places and for the most part, as soon as I can get home and check for mail, I get on over to Floral Court.

In the weeks we are in Louisville we are together except for perhaps two or three evenings. She once wants to go to a movie with a girlfriend from work. I feel left out. I think that I will go somewhere on my own, but I have no close friends at work since Paul left. There are several swell girls, but it would take an effort to try to arrange a date. I am still challenged by the lack of a car. Anyway, Juanita is the focus of my time and attention.

We still pretend that Mrs. Keegan is watching over her. When we go out, Juanita gives her a vague itinerary of where we will probably go and at what time we will return. One night we are downtown and see the movie *Sombrero*. I am really taken with the Flamenco dancing in the movie and want to see it again. Juanita worries that Mrs. Keegan will be sitting up waiting for her to return from our date. She goes to the lobby and telephones Mrs. Keegan and gets permission to stay to see the next showing.

We take all our meals out. I eat better than I did at home although my Mom is one of the great cooks. I would probably be gaining weight except for all the walking I do around the plant and on the streets. Juanita stays slim, too. We walk a lot. I don't know what she does for breakfast. Probably gets a roll or doughnut somewhere the same as I do. There are a good many places to eat downtown near where she works. I always get my food at the canteen. We are both counting our money. We are not frivolous in our spending. We are saving. We have the vague feeling that something more is coming.

*   *   *

W.J. Roe holding Glenna Ruth Hughes; sitting, Clyde Roe, Betty Sue Hughes, Snookie Roe, Jimmy Roe; on porch, Aunt Mary Liz McCord, Geneva Roe, Paul McCord, Nannie Roe, Perry Brown, Lillian Hughes, Odell Roe (1938)

*   *   *

Chapter 7

During the year between my graduation and when I left the farm to go to Louisville, Juanita and I began dating and her friend, Wilma Jo, started seeing Carl Watkins. We were appalled. He was 38 – she was 18. Her family was very protective of her and didn't want her dating at all. She gave them various excuses to be able to get out to see Carl, whom they didn't know about. She told them she was going to ball games or spending the night with a girlfriend and she would sneak away with Carl. She often used Juanita as her excuse. They rode the school bus together and Wilma Jo told her everything and took her into her confidence.

When we move to Louisville, Juanita stays in touch by writing. And one day Wilma Jo runs away from home and she and Carl come to us. I don't know the guy. I know it is going to make a lot of trouble for us. She and Carl are waiting on the doorstep when Juanita gets home from work. She says they are going to get married and find work in the town if they can. They are afraid of what her family might do. They need a place to stay the night.

I go by my house and ask Mrs. Shaw if it is okay to have a guest stay the night. She says it is. But longer than that I will have to pay for him. I meet them at the park and give them the news. Juanita has already cleared it with Mrs. Keegan to have Wilma Jo stay with her. We sit in Central Park and talk. Wilma Jo seems to be in shock at what she has done. Carl seems to be lost and childish. Maybe he regrets doing this, but they say that they are determined to marry. Tomorrow they will get the license and find a minister or justice of the peace. They worry that they will have to take a blood test and wait for the results before they can get the license.

I take Carl to my room and he has brought a very few clothes with him. He sleeps in his underwear. I'm not particularly happy sharing my bed with him, but I have grown up sleeping with Jimmy. He doesn't let the problems that beset him keep him awake. He goes right off to sleep, and isn't particularly noisy or noisome. In the morning he borrows my razor to shave. He is a grizzled old army veteran. And he has a two days' beard. I figure he will dull my razor. I only shave every other day and have a beard that is mostly peach fuzz.

He walks with me to the park and meets Wilma Jo there as they have arranged. Juanita is there, too, and is going to take them downtown and show them the courthouse. I am glad to turn it over to her and get on to work. I have my usual routine to follow. They can work it out for themselves. I suppose we will stay in touch with them.

But that afternoon when I go by to pick up Juanita to go eat, she says that Wilma Jo and Carl are waiting for us in the park. As they suspected, they have applied for a marriage license and have been sent to get a blood test. It will be a couple days before they will get the result and can go back to pick up the license. In the meantime they still need a place to stay. They have decided to stay on with us. I worry about having to pay Mrs. Shaw for the extra boarder in my room. They think it will be two nights at the most. I decide to try to slip him in without her knowledge.

So we stay up late until we think the Shaws will be in bed. Dr. Shaw has early morning hours at his office and they retire early. We tiptoe in and speak in whispers. We slip out the next morning undetected. I feel like a criminal. Carl takes his little bag with him. He says he will look for another place to stay. But that afternoon he and Wilma Jo are still around and we go through a repetition of the previous night's stealth.

The next afternoon I return to find that they are no longer around. Juanita has no clue. Wilma Jo has not left a note. We surmise that they have at last got their license, found a minister, married, and are now out of our hair for a while. Juanita worries about them and worries about the repercussions. Wilma Jo's parents, when they find out that she has come to Louisville, will likely blame Juanita for influencing her and encouraging her to run away. I hope that won't be the case. Wilma Jo is kin to me by marriage, and it isn't going to be pleasant to have a rift in the family because of this.

When we drive into town on Saturday afternoon, Pop likes to go out the old Bryan Station Road. He says it is shorter, but the real reason he likes to go that way is to look at the farms and the crops and the livestock and to record the general accord of things in his head. The road runs through some beautiful country and the farms are being improved as the country comes out of the big depression.

We always go to Paris on Saturday. When Mom and Pop first married, he worked for the railroad and they lived in Bourbon County near Escondida, and they got in the habit of going to Paris. Many of Uncle Harlan's grownup children live in the area and Mom still knows a lot of the people she had known when she lived in Escondida. They meet at the ten-cent store and talk. The corner of Seventh and Main is the center of town. The Newberry's five and ten cent store is on one corner, Ardery's drug store on another corner, and Lerman's clothing store on the third. The fourth corner has a non-descript jewelry store, but further along is Cook's and Kroger's grocery stores. On the same side as Newberry's is the A&P. Sometimes Mom and Pop do their grocery shopping on Saturday in Paris. In these days, before frozen foods, there is nothing to go bad. The only thing that can spoil in the hot car is if you buy a cut of meat or some leafy vegetables. We have our own meat hanging in the smokehouse and we grow our own vegetables.

Paris is a teeming mass of humanity on Saturday. We often have trouble finding a place to park. And as soon as we do Jim and I huddle with Pop who gives us money for the movie, and we hustle along the street anxious to see what is playing. There is always a feature and a western and the latest chapter of the current serial. Tickets cost eleven cents for kids. Jimmy is little and he is able to get in on a kid's admission until he is fifteen.

We get our five-cent bag of popcorn and candy bar and make our way down the aisle to find seats in the front row. We crane our necks upward to be close to our celluloid heroes and heroines on the big screen. I have been slow to adjust to movies. In these days before television, and isolated as we are on the farm, my first encounters with the silver screen frighten me. In the first grade I have to be taken out of a school showing of Alice in Wonderland. *The girl going down into a rabbit hole seems to be the worst kind of horror to me.*

Then Jimmy starts going to the Paris movie and coming out to tell me all about the pictures. His description of the Dick Tracy serial just starting makes me determined to try again. The serial is Dick Tracy Meets the Ghost. *I'm not crazy about the ghost, but I really look forward to the movie each week. Scary movies are still my bane. When scary parts occur, Jimmy has me close my eyes and cover my ears until the scene is over. Then he prods me, and I take up the movie again. It seems like they play a lot of scary movies on Saturday like* Frankenstein *and* The Secret of Dr. Renault *and* Wolfman.

What we really look forward to are good shoot-em-up war movies. Like Gung Ho *and* Wake Island *and* Back to Bataan. *The Japs always fall by the thousands. I hate Richard Loo with a passion. I think he would be killed on the street if he showed up in our town. Westerns we can tolerate, but they seem to have a sameness about them. We hate the singing cowboys like Roy Rogers. We really like the ones who are more action oriented like Hopalong Cassidy or the Three Mesquiteers. Republic Pictures is making good serials. Particularly, the ones with Kane Richmond like* Spy Smasher *and* Haunted Harbor. *I love* The

Perils of Nyoka *and say that if I ever have a son I will name him Larry after the hero in the picture.*

When they are ready to go home Mom will come into the show and come down front and collect us. She can barely see in the darkened theater, and we have to watch for her and catch her as she gropes about. Sometimes she comes before we have seen all of the movies and we beg her to let us stay a while longer. But if Pop is waiting, we have to go at once.

On the way back to the farm we go by way of the Paris-Lexington Pike. I like this way better, and we see some of Lexington. Sometimes he stops at May's store in the edge of Lexington for some reason or the other. This makes me happy, too. It delays us going back to the drab existence of the farm. I am still lost in the tinsel and glitter of the movies we have seen.

When I get back from the afternoon bank and mail run, Mr. Gerlach comes out of his office to meet me. All the girls in the office are watching. He says that the sheriff is there and wants to talk to me. The sheriff has filled him in that I probably know of the whereabouts of a girl who has run away from home. The authorities in Nicholas County have contacted the Jefferson County Sheriff's Office at the behest of her parents. He urges me to tell the sheriff everything or I will get into trouble.

The sheriff is waiting in a little office. He is a big red-faced man. He looks like a caricature of an ol' boy sheriff out of a movie. He is all business. He says that Wilma Jo's parents know she has come to Louisville. They are going to press charges against the man that has taken her away. They want her sent back and, if she is married, they are going to have it annulled.

He makes it sound ominous. I am glad that I don't know their whereabouts. I admit that they have been to see Juanita and me. I admit that Carl stayed a couple nights with me. But that was several days ago. They left and didn't tell us where they were going or what their plans were besides getting married. The sheriff doesn't believe me.

"You are telling me that these two people come to Louisville, and contact you and Juanita, the only two people they know in the town, and then just leave without telling you anything?"

"Yes. They were with us three nights, but we don't know where they are now."

"Well, where do you suppose they went?"

"I imagine they got married. And rented a room somewhere. And they are probably looking for work. Maybe you could find out if anybody has been hired on."

He withered me with a look for trying to tell him his job.

"Listen to your story. I don't believe it. And if I find out you are lying, you will be in a lot of trouble."

"I'm surprised that her parents told you to come to my place of work and question me about it. I had nothing to do with her running away. It may get me into trouble around here." Several of the girls can see into the office. He hasn't closed the door. But he doesn't raise his voice.

He ignores my concerns. "But they said there were going to get married?"

"Yes. They would have married the first day down here, but they had to get a blood test."

"I imagine it is done then. If they had contacted us right away, we might have been able to do something."

"It isn't as if Wilma Jo is underage or anything. I don't think they could get it annulled."

"I expect they just want to get her back home and work on her. Maybe make trouble for her man and try to scare him off."

He rises. The interview is over. I am relieved. What would I have done if the sheriff had come while they were staying with us?

"If they contact you, you call my office." He hands me a little card with a name and phone number printed on it. "That's me. If I'm not in, you give a message to the lady that answers. I want to know the minute they contact you. I'm thinking they'll be back in touch."

I think he is right. But if they are married, there is nothing that Wilma Jo's family can do. When she gets in touch with us, the first thing she needs to do is call her parents. They will have to accept it and call off the sheriff and his minions.

I go back to work sorting the afternoon mail. I keep my head down and avoid the stares of the office and switchboard girls.

The law in Kentucky is that all children begin school in September of the calendar year in which they reach age six. So in 1940 I am only five with my birthday in December when I start to school. Jimmy is almost three years older, but since he was born in February he is only two years ahead of me. Of course, Jimmy is much smaller for his age and old pictures show us as miniature twins. Thankfully, Mom and Pop quickly get over the urge to dress us alike. But Mom frets over our lack of growth and tries to get cod liver oil capsules down us. They gag me. Whenever I take pills she has to crush them in a spoon and give them to me with a drink of water and a spoonful of preserves.

Little though I am, I am cocky in school. I have gone armed with only a little of the alphabet taught to me by Mom. But I am a quick learner and never stumble over words in our readers. My handwriting is always atrocious, but by this time they have quit concentrating on the niceties of cursive writing. I am a plodder in writing. When I try to attain any kind of speed, my writing becomes illegible.

Bouts with mumps and measles and other childhood diseases cost me days at school. These aren't important except one period of over a month that I miss in third grade when we are learning division. When I get back to school, Miss Vermillion gives me special coaching to teach it to me. But I can't grasp it. I say I do but I don't. I pass from third to fourth grade not knowing how to do it. A month into fourth grade I go to Jimmy in despair, and he shows me how to do it.

I am small and blonde and have an angelic soprano voice. At Kenwick I am chosen each year to be in the Christmas play. This is really only a chorus that sings Christmas carols. We give one performance for the student body and another at night for parents and friends. When I am in second grade, we have to take a note home. They want us in choral robes. Mom has to buy cotton material and make me a choral robe. Mom knows just what to do. We carry lighted candles and march down the aisle. People ooh over me and reach out to touch my blonde hair. I am a star. But Mom and Pop don't come to school to see their youngest son in his triumph.

Miss Vermillion visits all her students at their homes. I bring Mom a message telling when she will be there. Our place is far off the road. Pop comes in from work to visit with her. He and Mom hold teachers in great respect. I stand beside Mom's chair and listen as Miss Vermillion heaps praise on me. Jimmy slides in beside a dresser and hides while she is there. When she leaves, Pop has me ride with her and get out and open the gates for her.

My best friend in the first grade is George Noble who rides the school bus with us. I love a little black-haired girl named Betty Gardner. Betty has no father. I don't know the circumstances. She lives with her mother on Liberty Road. Her mother sometimes works at May's store. One Christmas my father asks in front of Mrs. Gardner whether or not I have given Betty a present. I haven't. We chose names and I had picked another name. Pop has me pick out a present and Mrs. Gardner says she will wrap it and put it under the tree from me. Betty never mentions it. When I am in high school and have moved away, one of the girls in my class mentions that Betty is president of the regional council of students. She doesn't believe that I know her. I think about writing her a note to see if she remembers me, but I never do.

A week after the sheriff's visit, Wilma Jo calls Juanita and invites us out to the place she and Carl have rented on Broadway. It is a room up over an upholstery business. It is old and smelly and the furniture is worn and lumpy. It reminds me of the room I had looked at downtown the afternoon I first came to Louisville. The newlyweds are smiling and happy. Carl has found work. And Wilma Jo has called home and had a long talk with her parents. She thinks they are placated and reconciled to her marriage. But she has not given them her address. She will in a week or two. And if the reconciliation continues she will take Carl back to meet them.

We tell them about our encounters with the sheriff. They are apologetic for the trouble they have made for us. They had suspected that it might happen and it had been the reason they left without telling us. Now they are married and cheerfully looking forward to the future. Wilma Jo has been close to her mother all her life. I don't think she will want to stay long in Louisville. It has been a convenient place to escape to. Carl is a small town boy, too. He will want to go back to Carlisle and eke out a living there.

The room has a little stove and table. What people call an efficiency apartment. I know they are used to better. Wilma Jo wants to cook dinner for us. She opens a couple cans. She puts some hot dogs on to boil. I see roaches run under the stove. I'd rather eat out this day. But anyhow the boiling water should kill most of the germs.

They tell us about their search for a minister and finding a doctor for the blood test. They went to an old doctor that didn't have much of a practice. He was nearly deaf and they laugh about his difficulty understanding them and having each partially undress for his examination. They had given up finally on a minister and went to a justice of the peace.

We visit a while and go out and walk around the streets. Carl tells us about the job he has got at a grocery store. Wilma Jo hasn't found anything. I don't think she is looking very hard. It is traditional in our families that the married women stay at home tending to the house. The post world war boom of women working at various jobs has not penetrated into Nicholas County. But a sewing factory is about to open there that will employ a lot of women at low wages.

They walk us to the bus stop and wait with us until the bus arrives. Juanita and Wilma Jo make plans to get back together again soon. Their place is way out near 28th street. It is a long bus ride back.

Chapter 8

Around the plant there are a dozen little laboratories hidden in the warren of buildings. Small staffs in each of them work with polymers and resins and various bonding agents and dyes to try to perfect new types of lacquers and varnishes and enamels. These laboratories that had already been in existence before the new R & D building was built continue to function although the men in R & D have taken over a lot of their work. They are headed mostly by old-timers. Some of them have degrees in chemistry, but others have developed their expertise from years of serving an apprenticeship in the labs and later taking on more and more responsibility. Besides constant experimentation, they pore over all the latest literature and bulletins on their specialties.

Twice a day I duck up a dark staircase and find one of the labs near shipping. There is a small staff and they seldom have a mail delivery. One of my lunch companions, Joe Conniff, works here. Joe is one of those people who have previously held the mailboy job and has caught on here. I ask him how he came to get the job, and he says that he came by it by keeping in touch with the goings on around the plant and upon hearing of someone leaving, he went to the head of the laboratory and asked to be given a crack at the job. It seems to be a dull and dispirited occupation, but I know he is making probably twice what I am. Even though two jobs had been open the day I came to apply for work nothing has opened up around Jones-Dabney since except for the job in Accounting that Pauline got. Practically every job in the plant is either specifically for women or for men. There is no interchangeability of roles. There are no women salesmen or chemists.

Next to Joe is a little office where I drop off the mail when I have any for them. There works Lorna Leibowitz, the girl who has caught his eye and captured his heart. It is Lorna that Jimmy kids Joe about, saying that she is old and desperate and trying to hook him before her time runs out. Lorna is quiet and shy. She wears too much makeup, and I wonder if she is really trying to hide wrinkles and other signs of aging from Joe. She is nice and I think she is pretty. And I think she would be even prettier if she didn't wear so much makeup. She brings her lunch, but she and Joe do not eat together. I guess it is some sense of propriety that keeps them apart in their workplace. Lorna does not seem to have friends among the other women in the plant. She is Slavic I am told. She has a terrific figure, but she always seems withdrawn and kind of sad. I wonder what her dates with Joe are like.

I never talk about Juanita and me. I don't want to get myself kidded by Jimmy and the others. I don't know what they would say. None of them know her. Maybe there is something to be said for not dating girls at your work. But such a rule would be more for suppressing gossip than for any other reason. There are a lot of pretty girls at Jones-Dabney, but I am not a free man.

In our nation it is the great flood of 1927 along the Mississippi that is remembered and recounted in journalism and literature, most notably Faulkner's "Old Man." But for Kentuckians the most dramatic and devastating floods of the twentieth century occur along the Kentucky and Licking Rivers in 1937. Lives are lost, families are dispossessed, and livestock scattered. The cost in money and misery is countless. Unprecedented things occur along the courses of the rivers. The prisoners at the penitentiary in Frankfort are only moved just in time to save them. A new prison in LaGrange has to be built. The locks along the Kentucky are wrecked and have to be repaired.

Other homes wash away and have to be rebuilt. From that day on it is impossible to obtain flood insurance if you own property anywhere along the courses of these rivers. It is the result of years of denuding the hillsides near the headwaters of these streams and robbing them of their watershed. From that time onward a series of dams are planned and built along the rivers and the streams that feed them. Throughout the rest of the century there is talk of a great dam at Falmouth that will back the Licking up as far as my Uncle's place at Abner's Mill. And the local citizenry rises to fight it even though they continue to periodically suffer springtime flooding although not as severe as the one in 1937.

The rains come and settle in. The radio reports the heavy rainfall in the mountains and the steadily rising water. They give reports as record levels are achieved in Jackson and Beattyville. Uncle Joe and Aunt Matt will need help to save their farm tools and furniture. We get in the Pontiac and go to their aide. The bridge at Blue Licks will be under water so we go around by Carlisle and Cowan. Even so, coming down the hill along Buchanan Creek we can see where the Licking is backed up into the side creeks.

Uncle Joe is glad to see us. Glen and Homer have not been able to get time off from their jobs at the auto plant in Cincinnati. They have been there the night before and helped move some things and secure the house, but they have to return that morning to be at work. He doesn't know if they will be able to come in again, but he expects them since their boyhood home is in danger. Some neighbors have been in. They have taken the cow and horse and wagons and tools to their farms. All of Uncle Joe's farm lies low along the Licking. None of it is safe from the flood. In past years they have jacked the house up and moved it as close to the Licking Road as they could. But each year the floods seem to be more severe. The neighbors have already moved the furniture upstairs. The cook stove has been left unlit since breakfast and it has cooled enough to allow it to be taken up as well. Uncle Joe takes stout plowline and chains and ties them to the house and to the piles underneath and runs them to nearby sycamore and oak trees that have withstood floods in the past. If the water runs swift around the house they will take strain against the current.

Just now the river stretches out across the valley. It is noisy but deceptively calm along the edges. It has crept into the yard and during the day it relentlessly moves toward the house. Aunt Matt and Uncle Joe don't want to leave yet. Glen and Homer have come back without their families. There is nothing to do but watch and wait for now. Glen and Homer go back early to get some rest. We decide to stay the night. The adults will not sleep, or will sit around in the kitchen chairs that are the only furniture left downstairs, or sleep on blankets thrown around the walls. We kids are put into bed upstairs. Before we retire Mom takes Jim and me out on the back porch to pee before we go to bed. She allows us to stand on the porch and unzip and pee into the Licking River lapping at the piles under the house.

The next morning Glen and Homer come back. Clyde and Odell stay. Pop puts the rest of us in the car and drives us back to Lexington. He checks on the farm animals and ascertains that Perry has done a good job tending to things. He then goes back down to the river. He is gone again that night. The radio continues to report the widespread flooding although the crest passes town after town.

Pop and Clyde and Odell return the following morning. The river is dropping. It has gotten into the rooms on the first floor and left a residue of smelly river mud that will have to be cleaned away before the house can be reoccupied. Uncle Joe and Aunt Matt are relieved at their good fortune. They have had to clean up the mess in past years as well. The house always smells like old river mud and rot. When we go down there a couple weeks later, everything looks the same as it ever did.

For Juanita and me, our focus on Louisville is centered up and down Fourth Street. Every city has its main commercial street. These are often named Main Street or Broadway. In Louisville Main

Street is down by the water. A hundred years before it had been the center of commerce as the riverboats plying up the Mississippi and Ohio Rivers delivered goods for the merchants of the town and picked up tobacco and produce that had come in from the Bluegrass or the mountain region to the east. Warehouses had been piled high with these imports and exports. The mean streets around there had been named the "Cabbage Patch" celebrated in Alice Hegan's story of Mrs. Wiggs and her brood. The town has grown out from the river and Main and Market have fallen into urban blight. Commerce is now centered along Fourth Street that leads away from the water running out toward the new airport and to Iroquois Park at the extreme southern end of the city.

Juanita is a country girl, too, and doesn't mind some walking. But her shoes are not as sturdy as mine, and we don't often walk all the way downtown from out near Central Park where we live. Sometimes we walk just as far going one place or another if there is no hurry, and we can wander along talking about our work or news from home. Neither of us ever telephones home. It is not the thing to do in 1953. You have to connect through numerous operators. It sometimes takes a half hour for your call to go through. We both write letters home. There is little to tell our families, but to assure them that we are okay and to tell them when we will make our next trip home.

A little farther up Fourth Street are the big department stores and restaurants and movies. It is a bustle of activity. Like the downtowns of Lexington and Paris. In the early 1950's TV has not affected the habits of people who are used to going downtown to the movies on Friday and Saturday nights, and suburban malls have not pulled away shoppers from the concentration of stores between Market and Broadway. There are multi-story department stores. I have never been in one before that was not all contained on a single floor. It is like *Miracle on 34ᵗʰ Street*.

The center of the city's social life is the Brown Hotel at Broadway. Since its opening in 1923, along with the Seelbach, it has been regarded as one of the premier hotels of the city. It has a Georgian Revival style exterior and is faced with brick and stone and terra cotta. We look inside and see high ceilings with intricate plaster moldings and marble floors. The lobby is gracious and very European replete with antiques and oriental rugs. It is furnished in English Renaissance with polished brass and mahogany and oak accents. It is redolent of courtly charm and Southern hospitality. We pretend that we have come to buy something at the lobby shops and sneak looks around while trying to avoid the attention of the desk clerks.

Our explorations are usually centered up and down Fourth Street or other places where the Louisville transit system runs. It would be nice to have a car, but I am not ready to undertake that expense yet. We are saving our money. Riding buses is a pleasant way to get around. Almost like having a sightseeing company taking you around and showing you the town.

In the fall of 1931 Mom and Pop took their little family down to the farm to visit their Uncle Harlan. Out of the city the children ran barefoot through the fields, harassed the livestock, and ate tomatoes off the vine. When they were back in the city less than a week Robert (7) became ill of some mysterious malady and Lloyd (2) soon followed. Doctors were perplexed and could not make a diagnosis. Despite the efforts of the doctors and nurses and the resources of the big hospital, the boys died within a week of each other and were buried in Highland Cemetery near Ft. Mitchell.

Before the war Mom and Pop visited the graves occasionally, but with the war, gas rationing, and the fact that they now live a considerable way from Ft. Mitchell and Covington, they have not visited there in several years. In these times Decoration Day is the occasion to visit the graves of loved ones. You take a picnic lunch and eat under a shade tree and meet others whom you may not have seen all year when they too show up at the cemetery to place flowers on their loved ones' graves.

Mom wants to go back and decorate the boys' graves and Pop saves up his ration stamps. He buys a pint of whiskey to fortify himself for the long drive. The only time I ever see Pop drink hard liquor is on the drives to Ft. Thomas or later to Cincinnati. He makes it seem that it is a Herculean effort to pilot the automobile that considerable way through Georgetown and Williamstown and past the traffic that he encounters. We three younger children have no recollection of having visited the gravesites before. It is a new adventure to us, although we would rather be going to see Glenn and Lillian in Cincinnati. We are restless on the long drive.

At the cemetery Pop and Mom can't find the graves. They have to go to the little office and have them look up the records. Mom writes it down so that we can find them in future years. They are buried in a special children's section of the cemetery. The boys had died within a week of each other, but another child had died in the meantime and was buried between them. She takes scissors and trims the grass and decorates with paper flowers that she has made from crepe paper and wire. Mom and Pop decorate quietly. Their tears over their sons have long since dried.

We haven't brought a picnic. Pop knows a fellow who is an old buddy of his from the war and now owns a restaurant on the way back. We stop and they have a glad reunion. He cooks hamburgers for all of us. Mom has scared me in the past talking about people who have gotten food poisoning from bad meat in hamburgers. I am afraid to eat mine. Pop is pretty ticked off at me because I can't tell him the reason I refuse to eat the hamburger. It is like I am insulting his friend. Finally, they fix me a cheese sandwich which I devour. Pop eats my hamburger. You don't waste meat during the war.

We collect Wilma Jo and climb aboard the Broadway bus and ride it to the end of the line at Fountain Ferry Park. The park is at the western terminus of Broadway. The name has been bastardized from Fontaine Ferry, a passenger and auto ferry that plied the Ohio between Louisville and New Albany earlier in the century. A great deal of shaded parkland was left along the river here. No one dared develop it because of the danger of flooding. Now dams and locks and levees have tamed the river. The Army Corps of Engineers have done their job. The river has not flooded here since 1937 and probably never will again. An amusement park has sprung up here.

Fountain Ferry is not an imposing recreational facility. It is segregated, of course. But that is little spoken of around town. It is not "The Place To Go" on July Fourth as is Coney Island in Cincinnati or even Joyland Park in Lexington. There is a beach, but few people venture into the muddy and tainted river. The rides are not of colossal size. They are little larger than carnival rides in some cases, and the park is only starting to assume a permanent air.

We walk onto the grounds. It does not cost to gain admission, but one has to buy tickets to get on the various rides. We try to find things we all three want to do. We want Wilma Jo to have a good time. She has barely left the apartment since she and Carl married. He would not come with us. They are saving their money. They are having a hard time making ends meet. Wilma Jo is going to be very careful about what she spends. We will probably mostly walk around and look at the crowd and maybe have a hotdog and ride one or two things.

Then we discover that quite by accident we have come on Pepsi night. You can buy tickets for the rides or you can offer up Pepsi Cola bottle caps to gain admission. Some kids have brought paper sacks full of bottle caps that they have been saving up. When we find out about the promotion, we look around and see numerous bottle caps lying about. In a few minutes we have collected enough to get aboard the roller coaster. I have never ridden a roller coaster before. The one at Joyland Park is often closed because of its dangerous condition. I am not sure I should be on this one because of my heart. But I am game to try. Juanita and I share a seat and Wilma Jo gets on just behind us and chatters away. She has forgotten her squalid little apartment for a while. She darkly predicts that we will all die as the cars climb up to the first plunge. She knows that it is my first roller coaster ride. She is trying to get my goat.

The ride takes my breath away, but after the initial drop it is just a series of swift turns and mild dips. I enjoy having Juanita beside me. She does not squeal like some girls will do. But we are all happy and laughing when we climb down and go off looking for more bottle caps. Others are doing the same as we are. Just picking up bottle caps from the ground and around the fence. They must sell a lot of Pepsi at Fountain Ferry Park. Of course, no one prevents you from bringing your own drinks in.

I have never noticed how the ground in these places is littered with bottle caps. There is also the occasional cigarette butt, but these will dissolve eventually under the bombardment of the rain unless they are of the new filtered cigarettes. Bottle cap night is a good way to get some of the litter cleaned up around the park. The ground has gravel mixed in for those occasions when it rains and it cannot be swept. Litter is usually just raked up and the bottle caps slip through.

We soon collect enough caps to go on some of the other rides. We are riding a lot more than we expected to. This is not costing anything. Bottle caps are plentiful and we pick them up easily. Of course, we have to buy our hotdogs and sodas. We get Pepsis since they are having a promotion and are selling them for a dime. And we can use the bottle caps. The hotdogs are our supper. I have come straight from my work and met Juanita and Wilma Jo downtown.

The crowd thins out. People have to get home to sleep so they can go to work next day. We reluctantly decide we should be going. Carl does not expect us to be gone this long. Juanita and I have been keeping late hours since she came to town. We pay for it when we have to rise early. But it is always hard to say good night. I can see why it would be sweet to be married and you could just climb into bed and hold each other until sleep came.

At Wilma Jo's bus stop we get off with her. It is a bad part of town, and we don't want her walking to her apartment alone. We will have to pay another fare to get to our houses. There are no connecting lines where we could use a transfer from here. Wilma Jo and Juanita are animated and they walk along chattering happily. It has been good for them to get out and spend time together. For this time it is like they are schoolgirls again. They make vague plans for us to all have dinner sometime soon. She and Carl are going back to the farm to have him meet her parents. They have written and she has called down there. They want their daughter back. They will accept her marriage.

We do not have electricity in the big old ante-bellum house in Fayette County. It is hard to believe that the house was never updated. Even the meanest tenant houses and Negro shacks around there have electricity. We light lamps at night that cast such a dim glow that they are almost impossible to read by. Mom keeps her perishable food in an icebox that we have to purchase 100-pound blocks of ice for at town. And we listen to a big Atwater-Kent radio that has a removable battery that has to be taken out and taken to town to be recharged. We kids are not allowed to touch the radio, and our requests to listen to certain programs are often denied to conserve the battery.

The radio is our principal means of entertainment. We are a reticent family and hold conversations to a minimum. Although we kids have heard interesting things at school, we are not encouraged to speak. My father believes in the adage that children are to be seen — not heard. He and my older brothers are in the field all day. The radio is my mother's chief companion. She listens to soap operas as she goes about her work. On ironing day she sets her board up where she can hear the radio. She heats the irons on the coal-fired kitchen cook stove. When an iron cools she has to put it back on the stove and get a new hot one. Everything we wear is cotton and has to be ironed.

Each of the soap operas is fifteen minutes long. They start in the morning, but she mostly listens to afternoon soaps in the interest of battery conservation. She keeps up with ten or twelve of them. At suppertime we hear the news and listen to other fifteen-minute family comedies such as "Lum and Abner," and "Jack and Lena." Sometimes "Amos and Andy" or "The Johnson Family" are on. These are shows about Negros that are very comical. My father likes them a lot. When he takes us to a carnival he always looks for the minstrel show — he calls it the "nigger plantation."

At night Pop listens to comedy shows. We are on Central Time and the shows come on an hour earlier here than in the East. That is good because we have to go to bed early and get up early. On Sunday we hear "Bob Burns," "Jack Benny," "Edgar Bergen and Charlie McCarthy," and "Fred Allen." By the time "Fred Allen" comes on, I am in bed, and I lie there and listen to him as he takes his weekly stroll down Allen's Alley. On other nights there are "Baby Snooks," "The Great Gildersleeve," "Blondie," "Burns and Allen," "Bob Hope," "Fibber McGee and Molly," and "Henry Aldrich." Pop won't listen to dramas or detective shows. Later, when we move to the house at Hooktown and get a second radio, we go in the kitchen and listen to "Suspense," "Inner Sanctum," "The Shadow," and "The FBI in Peace and War."

On Saturday morning we have kids' shows like "Let's Pretend" and "The Buster Brown Show" with Smilin' Ed McConnell and Froggy the Gremlin. Jim and I like one called "The Adventurer's Club." Later, we hear "Corliss Archer" and "Archie and Jughead." We try to keep up with "The Lone Ranger" and "Superman," but they are always pulling those shows off the air.

On Saturday night we tune in to "Truth or Consequences" to see what Ralph Edwards is up to. Art Linkletter starts up a copycat program called "People are Funny." There are quiz shows. But the best is "Take it or Leave it" where people try to get to the sixty-four dollar question. Cigarette companies seem to sponsor a lot of the programs.

Television, when it comes, is like something from out of the next century. Pop lives to see it and looks forward to the day when he will be able to watch the Cincinnati Reds' ballgames. But he never owns a television set. He and I lean close and listen to Waite Hoyt call the games in the distant ballparks and use our own imaginations to picture the crowd and action on the field.

* * *

Showing off work horses, Perry Brown, Odell Roe,
W.J. Roe, Clyde Roe, Paul McCord (1938)

* * *

Chapter 9

Juanita meets me at our usual place in Central Park after I leave work. There are shady trees here and a bench where she can wait. It is across the street from Floral Court where she lives. I always try to be prompt, but sometimes I am detained by an unexpectedly heavy mailing or some other crisis around the office. It has to be a big crisis to affect me. As a lowly mailboy I am not likely to be the savior of Jones-Dabney.

Juanita is standing alone and is looking glum. She doesn't want to go to the drug store over on Oak where we usually eat. We walk back around by my house and over to Seventh Street and go into Tony's. Tony's is a small neighborhood restaurant. It does a small volume business and depends on neighborhood regulars to keep going. I have never been here in the middle of the day, but I expect they get some of the railroad people in. There is a switching yard not far away. I have discovered it only because I cut around this way in the afternoons coming home from work.

We have the restaurant all to ourselves. There is a girl waitress, and I guess that Tony is in the kitchen doing the cooking. It sounds like an Italian restaurant, but it serves typical quick-order fare. We don't look at the dinners, but instead order from the sandwich menu. While we are waiting for our orders, she gives me the news she has been wanting to tell me.

"I got my call from the FBI today."

The news hits me like a bolt of electricity.

"You did? You mean the call to come to work."

"Yes. I'm supposed to report to their headquarters in Washington in two weeks. Only a week and a half now."

"Did you actually get a phone call or did they send you a written notification?"

"They sent a letter to the farm. Auntie called Mrs. Keegan and she took the message. Auntie got her excited about it and she called me at my work."

She still doesn't look as happy about it as I would have. Washington – think of it.

"Boy, that's great. Just what you were waiting for. What we were waiting for."

"I hoped that they would hire me on here in Louisville. The agent told us that most of the jobs were in Washington. They need people there, but they hire a few for the office here."

"Still, it's a good opportunity."

"I don't want to go and leave you." She looks near tears.

"Well we've talked about that. I can try to get on, too."

"But it would be months. Even if they are still hiring."

"That's not bad. How long did it take you? Three – four months?"

"Something like that. Couldn't you come on now? You could find other work up there."

I consider that for a moment. I wouldn't be giving up such a great job at Jones-Dabney, but I remember all the trouble I had the day I came to Louisville interviewing around to find something. I haven't saved up much money yet, and her family wouldn't be happy about me going along with her.

I am still pondering when the food comes. She doesn't eat with much of an appetite.

"I don't want to go up there. If I just don't report to work, it'll be okay."

"But they went to all the trouble of doing the investigation on you." Neighbors have told the family of being interviewed by an agent on Juanita's background and character. They are careful whom they hire on.

"Yes, I'd feel bad about all the trouble they went to."

"What about your family? Don't they want you to go?"

"I don't know. They probably don't want me so far away. Of course, Allen will be delighted. If he thinks it will break us up."

"It won't break us up. We can write all the time like we did back in high school." When she was still in school and I was on the farm and we were dating, we wrote letters back and forth and my sister was the letter carrier. It was like having an express postal service. Now, it will be a couple days before letters will arrive.

"It's not the same. It'll never be the same again as it has been here this summer."

"But it could be good in Washington. You go on up there and get me an application. I'll be up to join you in no time at all."

She is not sure. She had almost forgotten about the application. She didn't think the day would come when she had to make a decision. I wouldn't have to think twice. It is a great opportunity. I have to talk her into it. She forgets her hamburger and stares at her plate. Tony leans across the counter and watches from the kitchen. He wonders at first if something is wrong with the food. And then he sees her glum face and my attempts to be upbeat. A lover's quarrel, he thinks.

I first become aware of the impending move while hearing Pop and Perry talk about it at the dinner table. We have lived as tenants on three different places since we moved back to the country. We have been with the Lebus brothers the longest — seven years, but Pop wants to work for himself and keep all the fruits of his labor — not share them with a landlord. He has gone to a realtor in Carlisle who has shown him several farms. When he finds one that he likes, he shows it to Mom also. He has to have her concurrence on the house and the kitchen. It is hard to imagine that a place could be less pleasing to a housewife than the house we live in on Lebuses. Old and without electricity, or running water, or a telephone.

They settle on a house in Nicholas County although it is just over the line from Harrison County where I was born. Mom is reluctant to go and I am appalled. We are moving toward the mountains. We have always looked down on people from Nicholas County. Uncle Lora tries to build it up. He wants us to move and be near him. He touts the big new school at Headquarters that we kids will be attending. I can't imagine going anywhere else after Kenwick.

Pop and Perry are excited about the move. They have already talked to other farmers in the area. They will take on a second crop on a nearby farm. It is wartime and help is scarce, but they think Jim and I will soon be able to help, and Perry will get his brother Herb and others he knows from Lewis County to come up and help during busy times. Pop makes big plans. He will have everything running smoothly by the time the boys are home from the war and can help out. He forgets Odell is married now.

They start to move some things to the new farm. We will go around the first of March. It is customary for farmers to move at that time of year between the finish of the previous year's crop and the start of the next. Pop takes us to Carlisle where he meets a last time with the realtor and the man he is buying the farm from. Mom and we kids wait in the car. I don't like Carlisle. It seems pretty dead compared to Lexington and Paris. We are moving into the boondocks. Mom is reconciled to it. We kids have no say and know better than to voice our objections to Pop.

We attend the last few days at Kenwick and say goodbye to our teachers and friends. We try to look on the bright side. Jim and I will have a new farm to explore although it is much smaller than the Fayette farm. The house we are moving to is newer than the Lebus house although it is frame. And it is electrified. We will have lights like our other relatives. And we won't have to conserve the batteries in the radio anymore.

After we move to Hooktown the first thing Pop does is go to town and buy a sack full of 40-watt light bulbs. He goes through the house and replaces every bulb with these dimmer bulbs. They still seem to shine like the sun to us.

Just across the river is Jeffersonville. You can see the lights over there when you stand at the foot of Fourth Street. We have talked about going over there some night. Our nights together have run out. The night before Juanita leaves for the FBI we decide to walk over there and see the town.

There is a long highway bridge running off of Second Street. It has a pedestrian walkway along one side. The bridge arches upward but not severely so. It doesn't have to accommodate ocean-going ships, only the barges and riverboats that ply up and down here. Its height is not a problem for me. A higher bridge would stimulate my acrophobia – fear of heights.

It is still daylight when we cross. Now in mid-July it doesn't grow dark until about nine o'clock. But it takes much longer to walk across than we thought. We could have caught a bus over. They cost more than a Louisville city bus and only serve as a shuttle picking you up in downtown Louisville near the bridge and letting you off somewhere in Jeffersonville. We don't know how much one will cost, and we don't want to be let off in some area of Jeffersonville far from the bridge. We are only going over for a quick look. We have to be up early next morning to catch the Greyhound bus to Paris.

"I'm glad I didn't buy a lot of stuff down here. I am barely able to get everything back."

"When we get to Paris, we can check everything behind the counter. Then move it to your car when the family arrives."

"Yes. I am still going to have to repack and sort out the things I am taking to Washington."

"Won't you need the same things you had here?"

"Pretty much. But in packing up I found some things in the drawers that I have never used. There's no sense dragging all that stuff to Washington."

I think she means there is no sense in her having to lug it around. If I were along doing the lifting, it would be another story. She has left me her record player, and some of her records. She is taking the others home. I am going to buy a couple new songs that I like after she leaves.

"Are you looking forward to the flight?" She is flying out of Bluegrass Field on Sunday.

"Oh, yes. I never thought I would be on a plane."

"You'll be there in what? Two or three hours?"

"We have a stop in Charleston. That takes about an hour. Flying time is less than two hours."

I think of our Senior trip to Washington that left by train in late afternoon and arrived the next morning. It seems impossible to make that long trip in such a short span of time. The train doesn't run up there anymore on weekends. If I went I would probably have to go by bus. It is a killing 22-hour trip.

"And have they told you what to do when you get there?"

"They gave me a number to call. Then they will send me somewhere for the night. And they have a list of apartments or rooms to rent to help you find a place."

It seems the FBI has the welfare of their employees as a priority.

"I'm hoping to find some other girls to live with. We can rent an apartment and do the cooking ourselves. It'll save a lot of money on food. It's ridiculous to eat out all the time like we have to do here."

It seems like we have a lot of things to talk about still. There is the old joke about the couple that got married whose main worry was that they would use up all their conversation in the first few days and wouldn't have anything to talk about in the years to follow.

On the Jeffersonville side it is not as built up as it is over on the Louisville side. It is mostly residential with a couple gas stations and stores. It is more like the neighborhood down around Central Park. We stop in a couple of the stores and look around disconsolately. We are finally attracted to a large building down near the bridge. We have seen its lights from the other side of the river and wondered what it could be. It is a large warehouse-type structure and inside it is partitioned among several shops. It is almost like a mall or something. One little shop sells household items; another has rugs. There is furniture in another and hardware elsewhere. It is a good idea, I think, to have all these various shops under one roof. But we are not buying anything. There is a jewelry shop. I would like to get Juanita something as a parting present. But she says she doesn't want anything, and I am afraid to ask the prices. Wouldn't it be nice to just choose things you liked and purchase them and not have to worry about the cost?

We can't find where the bus originates and start walking back across. No bus passes as we are walking. This late at night they don't run as often. We have stayed longer than we expected to. We catch a bus at the foot of Fourth Street and ride back to Central Park. We are talked out. It is the last time we will be downtown that summer. We feel like it is the end of something.

After moving to Hooktown, we don't want to go to the new school. We move on Monday, but we kids decide that we will take the week off. We see the school bus come by at morning. On Tuesday the driver pauses at our gate and waits to see if we are going to come out to ride with him. On Wednesday he blows his horn several times and waits on us. Betty Lee Harney, who lives across the road, has told him we are there. We are being offered a ride. Pop asks us why we are not going to school. We beg him to let us have the week off. But he tells us to get started by Friday and so we are out to meet the bus then.

Betty Lee, who has been up to see us, comes running up the road to stand with us and wait for the bus. She says the bus driver is named Brother Tanner. He is a preacher at the Saltwell and Headquarters Churches. The bus that picks us up runs down to Hooktown and then picks up children on the way back to Headquarters. He runs up Hardy Pike first and then picks us up since we live along the state road that runs between Hooktown and Headquarters. Then he has to pick up along Dogwalk Pike that runs back to Morning Glory. The far ends of Hardy and Dogwalk are in Harrison County.

We get a warm greeting from Brother Tanner and the other children on the bus. The bus is an older style with a flat roof, unlike the modern new one we rode to Kenwick. The seats are long benches down each side and in the middle. Betty Lee is between Colleen and me in age. She says that she will be in my room since I am in the fourth grade and she is in the third. Two grades are in each room.

Headquarters is a big bustling school, but not as nice as Kenwick. For one thing the floors are wooden. At Kenwick they were marble. Junior high and high school students are in the school as well. People are going every which way. It is no trouble finding our homerooms. The first eight grades are in the four rooms on the first floor. The other grades are upstairs.

I say hi to some of my new classmates who want to show me around, but I decline their urging. I wait just inside the doorway clutching my notebook and lunch box. The students don't look much different than those I went to school with in Fayette County, but I have convinced myself that they are hillbillies. A red-haired girl covered in freckles takes a shine to me. She says her name is Betty Jo. I don't hear right. I think she says "Banjo." Who but a bunch of hillbillies would name their daughter "Banjo" I think. Betty Jo ignores her classmates who go out to play before class. She stays and talks with me. She wants to find out all about me. She asks question after question. I give her short answers and wait for the teacher to come.

She is called Miss Dorothy. Here at Headquarters all the teachers are called by their Christian names unlike at Kenwick where we called them by their surnames. When class starts, all my classmates introduce themselves. We are a little class of ten. There are a few more in the third grade class. My class sits nearest the windows in two rows. I am given an empty seat near the back. When classes start, it is clear that I am ahead of the others in my studies. I have never been called smart at Kenwick, but I quickly get a reputation here as being a smarty. At Kenwick we were punished if we did not have our lessons prepared each day, so if I have unfinished homework in the morning, I go to my desk and pour over my books. It is just a leftover habit. The others on their way out to the playground see me at my desk and are puzzled. No one here is punished for being unprepared.

I have two cousins upstairs in the upper grades. Aunt Naomi's son, Junior, who we have been told to call C.C., and a distant Hughes cousin. We are instant celebrities when it is found out that C.C. is our double cousin. He doesn't associate with us since he is an eighth grader.

We discover that some of the teachers know our family also. Miss Hazel Schwartz and Miss Alpha Brierly are from down in the Licking area of the county and know our parents. Miss Brierly is talking to other teachers and sees me coming up the hall. She says, "Look at this little man strutting along just like a Roe." I don't know her. How does she know me? I walk on puzzled.

The little airport, called Bluegrass Field, handles commercial airline traffic for Lexington and the central Kentucky area. It had earlier been a private airport but when several airlines wished to establish flights into Lexington, it had been expanded to accommodate them. Nothing large came onto the main concrete runway, and the desultory flights hardly disturbed the tranquility of the lush horse farms in the area including famed Calumet Farm just across the road.

Parking is provided right up to the little terminal building that has ticket counters for the three airlines – Eastern, Piedmont, and Delta. Juanita has already bought her ticket. It is one-way to National Airport in Washington. She weighs her luggage. She is allowed to take only forty pounds on the flight. When she packed, each member of the family had hefted the suitcases and estimated the weight. Her uncle is used to hefting fifty and sixty pounds sacks of cattle feed and fertilizer. He has estimated it pretty good. She is prepared to open the suitcases and remove some things if she is over. But the bags are within the weigh restrictions.

We are very early at the airport and take seats to wait. She and I cannot sweet talk in front of her family. We have said our goodbyes the night before in my brother's old Dodge parked out on Concord Road. This time is for her family. Airline flight is a mystery to her foster parents who wouldn't think of entrusting their lives to one of the cumbersome aircraft. We have arrived early. We watch as other people arrive and check in for the flight. You can tell the seasoned travelers and those like us who are unfamiliar with the airport and airline procedures.

We hold hands. It is a chaste act, but Allen and her uncle make the excuse to walk outside and look at planes that are taxiing or landing. Her aunt does not take the hint to leave us alone and worries and fusses about her trip.

"Give us a call as soon as you can."

"I will. But it probably won't be tonight."

"Call person-to-person and ask for Ruth. I'll say that she is out with her boyfriend, so we won't be charged for the call, but we will know you are all right. If you are having any trouble, place the call in the normal way."

"All right."

"Write us as soon as you find a place and send us your address."

"I will. And I'll be expecting a lot of letters."

"You can count on it," I say. We have been over this numerous times.

We are watching the clock. I have to get to the Greyhound station and catch the afternoon bus back to Louisville. I wish I was going with her.

"What will you do tonight?" she asks.

"Go get some supper at the drug store, I imagine." I don't even have to say what drug store. She knows.

"Will you go by Mrs. Keegan's and tell her I got away okay?"

"Sure."

"She got the room rented before I left. I'm glad. She needs the money."

I don't answer. We have talked about all these things before. We watch the passengers unload from the flight that has come in from Washington. They will take a little while and the plane will turn around for the return flight. I suppose that they do maintenance at night. There is a morning flight and an afternoon flight. I wonder if it is the same aircraft.

We walk outside to look at the plane that will take her on her journey. The Eastern Airlines DC-3 has its stairs down. It has a wheel in the rear and people enter and exit through the tail. It is the DC-3 that has made commercial flight feasible. During the war the air force used them as cargo planes – the C-45. They carried the material that won the war. They even flew over the Himalayas into China. The cabin is not pressurized, but it will only have to get up to twelve thousand feet or so to fly across the Appalachians.

They call the flight for boarding. Juanita has chosen a seat on this side of the airplane. We say goodbye and kiss briefly. Her aunt has lost her composure and is crying. She gets Juanita crying as they hug and she starts for the plane. She pauses at the bottom of the stairs and gives us a cheerful wave. We can see her take her seat and so we wait until the stairs are taken up and the plane rolls away. We wave and wave.

Driving back into town the Smiths and I are glum. Mr. and Mrs. Smith can tell by the way that Juanita and I have acted that we are romantically connected. They appraise me as a future son-in-law. Allen seems happy that Juanita has gone. He provides a happy chatter until they drop me at the Greyhound terminal on Short Street.

Chapter 10

1953 is a wonderful time. The country has thrown off the gloom of the depression and has lived through the desperate years of World War II. The papers have started using the words "baby boom" to describe the population explosion as service veterans return and start families. A housing boom goes with it as all these young families need places to live. Many are entrepreneurs and start new businesses. There is plenty of work for everyone. Sure, prices are up, but salaries rise to match the prices. People are working and spending enough to have lifestyles never seen before and saving enough to ensure their futures. We are in a "police action" in Korea to let the communists know that no one is going to take it from us.

During the war people have predicted that television would come in and be as big as radio. But no one predicted its consequences – that people would stay at home and watch Uncle Miltie and Lucy and would stop going to the movies to be entertained. But that isn't too evident in 1953. The growing population disguises the fact that not as many people are showing up in downtown percentage-wise. There still seems to be as many people on the street as ever.

During the war they said that there would be flying cars after the war. I guess Detroit realized how stupid that was. Plenty enough people are being killed on the roads as it is. There is no need having the maniacs flying around the sky and crashing into each other. Airline travel is just coming into its own and TWA and Pan American are blazing routes all over the world. Pan Am has abandoned its clipper fleet that before the war had landed in harbors and lagoons and had not required airports. Municipalities are glad to float bonds to raise money for airport facilities. No one wants to be left out of the twentieth century.

Out of the war have come advances in medicine and foodstuffs and packaging. And most of all – plastics. Isinglass and cellophane are disappearing to be replaced by clear plastic. Cheap plastic notions are appearing as combs, utility pans, and disposable knives and forks and plates. Even some furniture is being molded from plastic. Metal toys and bric-a-brac are disappearing. Penicillin and new antibiotics are putting infections into the low-risk category. Doctors claim to be close to finding cures for polio, ALS, and cancer.

Some people do not have the temperament to deal with the plentiful money and added leisure. Alcohol consumption is increasing along with smoking, although warnings are starting to surface about the effects of cigarette smoke on the smoker and those around him. A little is heard about some misguided people smoking marijuana. But not much of these kinds of drugs are coming into the country. And the treasury department is active in enforcing the drug laws. Marijuana grows wild in Kentucky, but I have never thought of trying to smoke it. I do not care to smoke at all. But my family has depended on tobacco for our livelihood.

Music is not exactly big band but the sound hasn't strayed too far. Tex Benecke has the Glen Miller band, Bennie Goodman is still around, and so are Artie Shaw, Gene Krupa, and the Dorsey brothers. Lawrence Welk tours and plays at ballrooms and dances. Frank Sinatra has died out but Vaughn Monroe has a big voice and there are the new kids like Steve Lawrence and Eddie Fisher who are going to keep that kind of music going.

Basketball is still my favorite sport. The University of Kentucky has been suspended for a year because of a gambling scandal. It seems like the game has speeded up and is being played at a more frenetic pace, but it is not yet a contact sport. If two guys contact, a foul is called. Footballers have the option of playing with a facemask or not. Linemen sometimes use them, but running backs mostly eschew them, because tacklers grab them to throw runners down. The University of Louisville is going to have a fine senior quarterback named Johnny Unitas to lead them in the fall.

It is always going to be like this, only better. Korea will end. With everybody working there will be plenty of wealth to go around. Japan and Germany and the rest of Europe are back on their feet, and we will not have to send so much aid. Israel and the Arabs will stop bickering sometime. There will be government help for poor people and the elderly. Blacks will get more rights and stop making trouble. The forty-hour week will become standard. It will be easier to travel and maybe someday it will be commonplace for anyone wishing so to visit the storied cities of Europe and Asia. The future looks bright ahead.

We have only been at the new farm for a couple of weeks. I am just getting comfortable at my new school. One morning I am feeling unwell. I have a temperature and don't feel like eating. Mom keeps me home. I lay around all day. She tries to get me to eat toast and bakes me a potato. I don't want them. She feels my head to gauge my temperature and worries. She has already buried two boys.

Pop thinks it is nothing and I will be better in the morning, but Mom prevails. They dress and load us kids in the Pontiac and we go to Paris to see Doctor Hart. He is our family doctor and he has paid house visits to us on the farm in the past. He has diagnosed mumps and scarlet fever and measles. But he is getting older and doesn't like to drive as far as Nicholas County.

Jim and Colleen are left in the waiting room while Mom and Pop go in with me and tell the doctor about my symptoms. If I were a quieter child, they might not have noticed. But I am usually boisterous and running about and would insist on going to school if I felt like it. The doctor removes my shirt and listens to my heart and takes my temperature. He turns me around and listens to my heart and lungs from the backside.

I dress and go out to sit with Jim and Colleen while my parents talk with the doctor. When they come out of his office they are glum and Mom is wiping her eyes. She has a sack of the purple pain pills the doctor hands out for everything. They are nasty and I will have to mash them up and take them with sugar or preserves. Anyway, I figure I will feel better tomorrow and be back in school.

They don't want to scare us, but realize that they have to tell us something. They say that the doctor says that I have rheumatic fever and a heart murmur. I will have to go to bed for several months. I am devastated. It will mean missing school. It will mean that I will be in bed throughout the spring and most of the summer. I won't be able to run over the farm with Jim and our dog, Pete. What a bummer.

I don't feel any worse when we arrive home than I have at any other point during the day. But this time Pop carries me from the car to the house. It is the only time in my childhood that I remember being in his arms. I have my arm around his neck. I smell his tobacco breath. I am sorry that I have caused trouble for him.

Years later I find that the diagnosis has been much more devastating than Mom or Pop let on. The sickness has badly damaged my heart. The doctor has told them they must keep me quite. Activity will place too much strain on my heart. They are to be prepared that I will probably not live more than two or three more years.

They evict Colleen from the baby bed she has slept in all her life. I am to sleep in the room with them so they can watch over me. I can't believe that they expect me to lie here for the next several months doing nothing at all.

Every year during my childhood I have developed a hacking cough at the onset of cold weather and it plagues me all winter. It plagues my family also who must listen to my hacking attempts to bring the phlegm up out of my lungs. I cough a lot at night. Jimmy learns to ignore it and sleep right on. But Mom can hear it and it worries her a lot. She has had a bout with tuberculosis as a young mother and TB hospitals are still in operation in the state and out west to deal with the disease. Mom takes me to Dr. Hart who listens to my lungs. He tells her that I have a cold in my bronchial tubes. These are the small branches of the lungs. He tells her it is from my sleeping in cold rooms. I need to sleep in a warmer room.

Only the sitting room and kitchen have fires in the winter. These are allowed to burn down or go out at night after bedtime. They are rekindled in the morning. Pop is not motivated to get up and tend the fire at night. They keep the door to our bedroom open for a while to let some heat penetrate before bedtime, but it is not effective. The bedroom is still chill, and I continue to have my cough and runny nose.

At least in the summer on the farm the cold and cough go away. I work under the hot sun and bake them out. But in the spring before I leave the farm I develop a bad cold. My throat becomes infected to the point that I cannot swallow, and I have to go to the doctor about it. He gives me a penicillin spray that clears up the infection in about a week. He tells me that when I get future colds I might develop throat infections. I am supposed to avoid colds.

A few weeks after Juanita leaves Louisville I contract a massive cold. The older knowledgeable ladies at Jones-Dabney say it is caused by running in and out of cold rooms. Some few of the offices have air conditioners as does the bank. It is heavenly to linger a moment in such places and cool my sweaty body. My body must not think it is such a good idea. There is nothing worse than a summer cold.

It goes straight for my throat, as I knew it would. I spray the penicillin into my throat and hold it at bay. Taking off from work never crosses my mind. The workers must get their mail. I trudge around and blow into my handkerchief. The cold persists. I don't know that you can buy cold medicine that will relieve it. One of my lunchtime companions tells me to go get rhinitis tablets. They will dry up the discharge coming from my nose and eyes. Dr. Shaw happens to be at home that afternoon. I ask him about rhinitis tablets. What does he think of them? He is non-committal. He doesn't think much of them, he says. I don't want to bother him for free medical advice. The pharmacist sells me rhinitis tablets without a prescription. I take a few of them. My runny nose dries right up. I think, why haven't I known about these all my life? I wouldn't have had to suffer every winter with the effect of colds. I am a happy boy. The cold goes away, and I save the rest of the rhinitis tablets against the day I contract another cold. It is like a miracle drug. The bottle does not have any information as to any harmful effects on my heart or renal system.

Mom sends a note to school that I have rheumatic fever and have been confined to bed. Miss Dorothy makes all my new classmates write me letters wishing for my recovery and for me to come back to class. Some of their writings are so shaky that I have trouble reading them or making out the signatures. I write them back thanking them for the letters and telling them I am better. Miss Dorothy sends my books home by Jimmy and sends me assignments to do. In Geography they are studying Norway. She has sent me a lot of questions about it. One asks me why skiing is so popular there. I am not familiar with skiing. I think she must mean skating.

I am soon tired of the little baby bed where I lie. I don't know why I don't crawl into Mom and Pop's big bed during the daytime, but it just doesn't occur to me. The baby bed has bars on it. I feel like I am in jail.

My fever has gone and I feel fine now and want to go back to school. But Mom and Pop are following the doctor's orders. I stay in the bed except to get up to use the potty. Every four hours Mom brings me a purple pain pill mashed up in a teaspoon and a glass of water and something to take the taste out of my mouth. Pop and Perry are busy putting in the new tobacco crop and corn and a second crop on a nearby farm.

Patsy Asbury down the road takes Jimmy and Colleen with her to Sunday School on Easter. They come home and tell me how nice it is. I have never been to Sunday School. I beg Mom and Pop to let me out of bed and go with Jimmy and Colleen next Sunday. Mom takes me back to the doctor. He listens to my heart again. He shakes his head when he hears the murmur. He says that I have to stay quiet, but he allows me to get up and move about the house. I am released from my jail.

We kids persuade Perry to take us to Sunday School the week after Easter. It is a small congregation. I enjoy it. We stay for church. Brother Tanner teaches against the evils of taking the Lord's name in vain among other sins. Perry is convinced the preacher has made his sermon just for him. He will not take us again. And Pop will not take us either, so my one visit to Headquarters Church is the sum total of my childhood religious instruction.

I still cannot go to school but at least I can follow Mom around. I listen to her soap operas with her. She teaches me how to make a cake. Yellow cakes are my specialty. With caramel icing. I am using up her sugar ration. But I keep us in yellow cakes.

It is clear that I am not going to expire anytime soon. I am allowed to go to school on the last day to pick up my report card. I am promoted to fifth grade. I have a glad reunion with my classmates. I am starting to get out some. Perry no longer has to stay with me on Saturday while the others go to town. I go with them and Jimmy fills me in on what has happened in the current serial – Junior G-Men of the Air. *I am slowly picking up my life again.*

I have to get on with my life. It is pleasant enough in Louisville in mid-summer. The sun blazes. I can feel it on my back and neck as I make my tour of the plant. The switchboard room is cool as I sort the mail and get ready to make my early afternoon run to the bank and the post office. As I walk along Hill Street the sidewalk shimmers and the buildings swim through a glaring haze. The town seems half asleep on these hot days.

With Juanita gone my focus is more on the job at Jones-Dabney. I have come to know the people. They are my family now. I have never been a talker, but common courtesy forces me to carry my side of the conversation whenever I stop in their offices with the mail. I start to learn a little about each of them whether or not I want to. And they draw information out of me. They know where I come from and the part of town I reside in and that my girlfriend is off in Washington.

With Juanita gone I play at being the martyr. I write every other night. Nothing ever happens and my letters have a sameness about them. Juanita talks a little about her work. She doesn't appear to have such a glamorous job as we expected. She says that all the employees where she works are mostly just out of high school. They are involved in processing fingerprints and identifying criminals by comparing new fingerprint cards that come in from various police stations about the country with old cards on file that match recent arrests to old crimes that are still outstanding. She says they run the place like they are all still in high school.

I have a hard time figuring out just what Juanita's life is like there. She has met a couple other girls and they room together. But they can't seem to settle on a place to live. Her address moves from Lamont Street to Kilbourne Street and to South Carolina Avenue. She says where she lives now she can walk to work. She formerly had to ride the trolley. I can imagine the trolleys and the bustle along the streets and the masses of cars moving down Pennsylvania Avenue past the monuments and White House and

Capitol. When I get up there we are going out every weekend and see all the things that I have heard about and read about all my life. Imagine being able to walk right into the White House and Capitol and Washington Monument any time you want.

She says that she has given my name as a prospect who would be interested in working for the FBI, but they have not contacted me. She doesn't say that they are particularly short of people, but the kids just out of high school get homesick and quit, so there is a constant turnover. Maybe they hired all they needed at the end of the school year, and as these new hires slowly dissipate, they will send out the call for more help.

I have come to Louisville because Juanita wanted us to come and I wanted to be with her. It doesn't make sense for me to be here without her. If the call from the FBI doesn't come through, how long am I going to stay? I might be able to get a better position with Jones-Dabney, but nothing has come up so far that I could handle. I could go to school at night at the University of Louisville and get a degree of some kind. I should look at Chemical Engineering if I want to stay at the paint company. I wouldn't be able to start until the next year. Then I would be two years behind my classmates who have come out of high school and gone on to college. I want to be in Washington, but I am keeping my options open for improving my position at Jones-Dabney. It never crosses my mind to go back to the farm.

We are raising a second crop on the farm of Mr. Cowell who lives on Collier Road on the other side of Hooktown. It is close enough that Pop and Perry can take our wagon, plows, horses, and mules over there and return them at night. But often they just leave them there to use them on the next day. The routine is to work several days there in the tobacco and then bring things back and work the next week or so in our own.

Perry's brother, Herb, has come up to help us. And he has brought another man along. The tobacco setting is going well and we are all happy in the little house. We kids are always curious about new people and Jimmy and I follow the new men around and ask a lot of questions. Perry has an old 1936 Ford that he has to park on the top of the hill each night. The starter doesn't work and he can roll it off and kick the engine over. He always has to park it on a hill. It is easy to start once it is moving. But it is a big bother when he wants to go to town. The man with Herb says he can fix it and they get under the hood and tinker and sure enough the motor engages with the foot starter.

Pop sends Perry over to Cowell's to pick up a singletree that they will need next day in our own crop. He loads the other new men in the car and takes Jimmy and me along. We stop at the Hooktown store and Jimmy and I get chocolate-covered peanuts. We eat part of them. We have to take the rest back to our sister, Colleen.

At Cowell's we drive across the field and leave the car. Perry no longer needs to park on a hill. We get the singletree and wave to Mr. Cowell and his Negro tenant, Mr. Johnson, who are pegging down canvas on their tobacco beds. Mr. Cowell waves and shouts and we wave back. Then we hear what he is shouting. He is gesturing toward the car. Flames are shooting out of the hood. The men run to the car and we kids are told to stand back. Perry is frantic. The engine is on fire. Mr. Johnson runs up with several sacks of straw that he has used to lay on when he was weeding the tobacco beds. He slices the ends out of the burlap bags and dumps the straw. Perry and Herb soak the bags in a mud puddle and apply them to the engine. Herb keeps asking if the gasoline tank is in the front of the car.

The mud puddles are more mud than water, but somehow the men get the fire out. The fire has probably been caused by the faulty starter. The others are shaky and sit down to watch the car for a few minutes to be sure the fire does not flare up again. They sit around and talk *about the fire and smoke cigarettes to calm their nerves. Jimmy and I have more chocolate-covered peanuts to calm ourselves.*

We cut across the farms to walk back home. It is not far when we walk across the fields and don't have to follow the road. The man that has worked on the starter carries the singletree. He feels bad about it. Perry wonders how he can get the car to town to get it worked on. Pop and Mom are surprised to see us walking in. Perry tells them what happened. Pop regards it as somehow Perry's fault. He is like another errant son to him. We sheepishly give Colleen the few chocolate-covered peanuts we have left. We try to explain that we had saved her a third of them until the fire happened. She is nearly eight now and starting to get smart-mouthed. "I suppose you had to eat them to save them from the fire."

*   *   *

Colleen, Nannie Roe, W.J. Roe, Lynwood, Jimmy (1943)

*   *   *

Chapter 11

A hundred years before, the area around Central Park had been out in the country. A 17-acre estate had once existed where Central Park now was. It had been owned by a clergyman who sold it to one of the DuPont family. The DuPonts opened the estate as a park in a moneymaking venture and lived among all the activity which included balloon ascensions, fireworks, and concerts.

During the Southern Exposition of 1883-1887, which was housed in a great hall just south of the estate, the entire grounds were thrown open to the public. It was said that 4600 lights, more than existed in any town other than New York City, were installed about the estate and exposition buildings, and were activated by Thomas Edison himself. An electric trolley circled the park and passed through an artificial tunnel during the years of the exhibit. Since the DuPonts owned the Central Passenger Railroad, which ran the trolley system on Fourth Street, they had the lines extended down to Magnolia Street in order to bring people to the park lands. Thus, when the estate later became a park it was named not for its central location but for the Central Rail line.

The city purchased the estate in 1902 and commissioned the famous landscape architect, Frederick Law Olmstead, the designer of New York's Central Park, the U.S. Capitol grounds, and the Biltmore Estate, to lay out the new park design. The residence was demolished, but some of the adjacent buildings, such as its carriage house, were moved off the parkland into the area around St. James Court. Olmstead designed a colonnade and pavilion for outdoor plays and entertainment. For some years a swimming pool operated in the park.

In 1953 it still retains its shaded elegance, but couples are seldom to be seen strolling its shaded paths in their Sunday best. It is all more informal now – a park for the working man and harried families with youngsters to entertain. The tranquility is disturbed by the pock of tennis balls meeting racquet and the bounce of basketballs on the one solitary court near St. James. Some daring young sun worshippers don bathing suits, spread blankets, and work on their tans.

I like to find a shady place, one where I can preferably watch the tennis courts. The game is new to me and I watch the graceful movements of the players. I am still used to my years on the farm where we avoided the sun as much as possible and hid from its harmful rays. It is pleasant sitting under the big trees, listening to the whisper of the breeze stirring the great limbs, and hearing the chatter of birds about their daily activities. Children run about under the half-watchful eyes of their mothers. Young girls in print dresses smelling like flowers pass by. A mower works nearby clipping the lawn to a smooth carpet finish.

Not long ago Juanita and I sat on these same manicured grounds. We talked and joked with Wilma Jo and Carl as we plotted our futures and whiled away the hours. I can almost see my house on Ormsby from here. Floral Court where Juanita lived is just across the way. It seems like my park. I take an interest in all the things going on.

In late March 1944, the prognosis for my devastating illness is a grim one. I am ordered to bed for several months and a death watch is instigated. By Easter I have battled my way out of bed, and by mid-May, the end of the school year, I am able to go collect my final report card and begin riding to town with the family on Saturday afternoon. Gradually, I am allowed to walk around the farm with

Jimmy, and when we are out of sight of the house, we are running and jumping as before.

Pop and Perry are struggling with the two crops. Pop is unable to find hands to help him set out the tobacco. Two black hands that he has gotten in Carlisle are worthless. He curses one and runs him off in the middle of the first day. He makes him walk back to town. The other finishes out the day and draws his pay and doesn't come back. It takes three people to operate a tobacco setter. One to drive the horses and two to drop the plants. In frustration Pop puts Jimmy on the setter with Perry. Jim's legs are so short they will not reach the closest setting of the footrest. Pop wraps a piece of wood on it so that Jimmy's feet will reach.

Jimmy is puffed up about getting to do a man's job, but it is tiring for a twelve year old boy to put in long hours on the setter. I follow the setter and set out plants they miss. I take the side of my bare foot and rake dirt to plants that are set shallowly in rocky and clay areas. I follow the setter all day in the hot sun. When they are near the end of the row and are about to run out of plants, I run ahead and grab a handful and bring them back so they can finish the row. I go to the house and bring back cool water for the others to slake their thirsts.

Later in the summer, as the tobacco grows taller, Jimmy and I are given hoes, and we work with others to cut weeds out of the tobacco and corn. I am too slow to do a row by myself, so I walk ahead and switch back and forth to help the others. I am allowed to take my time. Pop works ahead to operate the cultivator. Perry plows the corn with a mule and a five-shovel plow. He is not used to working with a mule and cusses it all day long.

In late summer our tobacco and that which we are raising on Cowell's farm is all maturing at once. Pop and Perry have gone through ours and topped it. After it is topped and it starts to spread, suckers appear between the leaves and stalks. These have to be wrung off. This is called suckering tobacco. It is slow work for each plant has five or six suckers that have to be removed by hand. Pop is working at

Cowell's with Perry. He starts Jimmy and me out on the lower side of our patch and tells us to work our way up the hill.

It is a hot day and I have not fully recovered my vigor from the weeks I spent in bed. Pop tells us we don't have to rush, but to keep at it and we will eventually get it all suckered. I try to take my own row but I am slow and it seems it takes forever to get across the field. We do better when we work in a single row. I go ahead and sucker the plants ahead of Jimmy. When he gets to where I have begun he comes forward to take my place and I move farther ahead. We are only getting two rows per round trip, but we are crossing the field rapidly.

On the farm we have plenty of milk. We have discovered that by mixing in Hershey's syrup and shaking it in a little bucket we can make the facsimile of a milkshake. We tell ourselves that after every couple rounds of the field we will go to the house and make ourselves a milkshake. We keep at it and try to make it up to a tree that has been plowed around on the lower side of the patch.

We do not quit until Pop and Perry come home and Pop calls to us to bring in the cows. We take our water bucket and walk in happy and tired. We think we have done a good day's work. Mom praises us to Pop and says that we have stuck to it all day. He asks if we have made it up to the tree. We proudly tell him we have gone two rows past the tree. He had been joking and meant the prominent tree at the top of the hill. When he finds out we meant the one on the lower side he is not overly pleased. He tells us to continue of the morrow. It is hard to face up to another day of the tiring work. The day comes when I have to quit because of exhaustion. Pop excuses me from the work and Jimmy goes with them to Cowell's. We never make it to the upper tree. Pop and Perry have to finish up.

A lady parks in the shade of the big oak trees alongside Sixth Street. She opens the car's back door and trunk and takes a number of items out. She gathers an armful and carries them purposefully into the park. She walks an uncertain course toward the colonnade and seems to be looking for a good vantage point. She deposits the things she has brought onto the grass and returns to her car for another load. If I knew her, I would offer to help, but in the city it is better to smile and leave people alone unless they come to you asking for assistance.

She gets the rest of her things and closes up the car. This time she has a folding chair and a tripod. Well, heck, I think, she had a canvas before. I believe that she is going to paint a picture. I am very curious but I don't want to get too close and be an annoyance. I move to a strategic place where I am still in the shade, can watch the players on the tennis court, and see what she is doing with the painting.

I have judged my location well. I have an oblique view of the canvas. It won't be obscured by her back as it would have had I not moved. She slips into a loose smock and looks darkly at the limbs over her head as if daring a bird to roost up there and violate her canvas. She arranges her paints, and I see for the first time that she has several jars of water with her. I also see that she doesn't have a canvas at all on the tripod. It appears to be a square of particle board. She pins a piece of paper to it. She is going to do a watercolor.

She begins to sketch the scene lightly with a piece of charcoal. At times she reaches up and smudges what she has drawn. She is making it very light so that the watercolor will cover it. The sketching does not take long. I think she just wants a guide so that her perspective will not drift off. There is a path between her and the colonnade that people come walking along. They see her painting and they detour to walk behind her and see the painting. If they pause it is only for a minute. They respect her as an artist and don't interfere with her muse.

Now she is applying the paints. Pastel clouds and trees and grasses are being splashed on the paper. She is as absorbed in the work as if she were an author guiding her characters through a particularly intense sequence of events in a novel. I wish I could see better. I decide that when I adjudge that she is nearly finished, I will stroll over and get a closer look.

My attention is split between the tennis matches and the artist. Other matters intrude on my thoughts – my work, plans for the upcoming week, and thoughts of the farm and Juanita far away. I allow myself to drift. The thwock of the tennis balls is like a lullaby. The twitter of the park birds is familiar and soothing.

I come back with a start. I have nodded off. The players have left the court. The lady is putting away her things. She stands and backs away from her painting and regards it critically. She looks at it from various angles as she wipes her brushes, and caps her paints and water jars.

I get to my feet and move toward her slowly. I am afraid that she will whisk the painting away before I get to look at it. She sees me and smiles and moves aside to let me look. She has concocted a confection of soft blurry colors. She has swirled whites and grays to emulate the clouds in a Vermeer blue sky. Blotches of green portray the trees and lawn framing the pinks and whites of the colonnade. It is disappointing to me that the colonnade is a series of indistinct pillars and columns and connecting piers. I am used to oil paintings that have more definition. But the overall effect is pleasing and soothing, and I think she has captured the essence of the scene.

I tell her I like it very much and offer to help her carry her things to the car. She will not trust me with her paint things. I take the chair and the tripod. She takes the case that has her paints and the board that still has the painting pinned at the corners. She is letting it dry before she unpins it. I ask to see it again before she lays it carefully on the seat beside her. I thought I had missed something before. Something that had tugged at my subconscious. Yes, there it was. On the bank below the colonnade she has brushed in a reclining figure. I look down at my shirt. The pastel rendering is very close. She has painted me into her picture while I slept.

Pop and Perry have bitten off too much. Raising two crops in the war years when farm hands cannot be found has proven to be folly. Pop always likes to get his tobacco stripped and on the market before Christmas. The sales continue on into March but the price often falls off after the sales resume after the Christmas break as the agents for the tobacco companies reach their quotas. Of course, there are the government price supports, but if your whole crop is sold at the price it is graded at, you will not make much unless you have pull with the man who determines the minimum bid. Pop does not.

We have our crop stripped and on the warehouse floor before Christmas, but the crop at Cowell's has yet to be finished. It will be into February before we finish up. Pop gets a series of men to help, but none proves satisfactory. He is resigned to a late sale. Perry, he, and we boys are going to have to do most of the stripping. The problem is that Jimmy and I can't come to the stripping room after school to help. The Cowell place is too far away. Jimmy is kept home a few days to help.

The holidays are a boon to Pop for he has Jimmy and me home for almost two weeks. He plans to make a good dent in the crop while we are available. Every morning we are up before dawn and have breakfast while Perry milks the cows. Mom packs us a lunch. We will not even take the time to drive home for dinner. We take the short ride through Hooktown to Cowell's. The stripping room is a little shed off the main tobacco barn. We bring the cured plants into the stripping room in great armloads and put them on a bench and strip the leaves from the stalks, grading them and tieing them with a leaf, and pressing the hands down tightly so that they can be handled and transported easily later. Jimmy and I can't grade tobacco well so we strip the tips and carry in the tobacco to be stripped and carry out the stalks. It is a poor way to spend our Christmas vacation.

We are making good progress. The tobacco has to be limber, such as is achieved on a rainy damp day, before it can be taken down from the barn, else the dry leaves will crumble and a considerable amount of it will be lost getting it down from the rails where it hangs in the barn. By Christmas Eve we have stripped up all the tobacco we have down. Pop frets over the lost time. But he knows that he can do nothing about the weather. We will be free to enjoy Christmas itself.

But Christmas morning arrives rainy and misty. Jimmy and I play with the toy guns we got. Pop jumps in the car and drives over to Cowell's to see if the tobacco is "in case." It is. We have an early dinner and have to put aside our toys. It is too good an opportunity to not take advantage of. Who knows if a wind might come up at any time and dry it back out again? We take down a mighty lot of the tobacco. Perry works on the rails of the barn dropping the tobacco down to my father. Jimmy and I run the stalks down the sticks and Jimmy pulls sticks for my father when he puts it in a bulk for stripping.

Pop wants to get as much down as he can. He doesn't want to be caught with available help again and no tobacco down to strip. He leaves us working in the barn and drives back to our house. He has Mom make us up a supper. We will work as long as we can. He brings back supper and two lanterns to illuminate the barn. But he doesn't want Perry up in the barn after it gets dark. They take down as much as they can. We slip the tobacco to the ends of the sticks and set it around to be sprayed and placed in the bulk later by lantern light. We cover every available foot of the barn floor with the dropped tobacco.

We stop for a few minutes to eat. Mom has sent sandwiches made with the ham that she has baked with brown sugar and with whiskey-killer cinnamon drops. She has put in slabs of the white cake and fudge cake that she has had a lady in town fix for our Christmas. She has tucked in some candy for us boys from the box that had been by the tree on Christmas morning. We drink from the shared water bucket. Our hands are gummy and black from handling the tobacco. The taste of the tobacco gum gets on our Christmas supper.

Jones-Dabney women are employed in a number of clerical positions. With the exception of the Accounting Department where Pamela Brown holds sway, all the others work under the direct supervision of men. They do not expect to go any higher in the company. That is just the way it is. The secretaries all seem content. Most are good typists and know how to take shorthand or work a Dictaphone machine. They have been smart enough to take these courses in high school, but there are a few business schools around where you can get instruction on these things. I have taken typing in high school, but Miss Brierly did not take any interest in seeing that I learned without looking at the keyboard, so I never became proficient. I wish I could type better and that I knew shorthand. They said that shorthand was a kind of cipher. I am always writing cryptic notes to myself that I don't want other people to read. Shorthand would be useful. But people probably can't read my writing anyhow.

There are only a handful of women tucked in the warren of buildings about the plant outside of the main administrative building. Some of these buildings are gloomy. The offices seem to have been framed in as an afterthought. It is almost like you have encountered a flower in a cavern when you find one of the secretaries housed back in a dark office. The main purpose of these buildings is to house the ingredients and provide the machines and vats where the various paints are mixed. Jones-Dabney can mix anything – lacquers, varnishes, enamels, polymers. We provide house paints, barn paints, porch paints, concrete paints. We have large accounts with auto companies and provide paint for their new cars. On any given day, dozens of trucks back into the loading dock at our shipping building and load up pallets of gallon cans or roll on 55-gallon drums. They pull out of the plant with their California or Massachusetts license plates advertising their destinations.

I move about through the alleys. Sometimes I have a letter, and I must ask in Personnel where the worker is located. I slip up back alleys and find doorways I never before knew existed. I cut through areas where the smell of ammonia is strong. I hold my breath till I get through the cloud. In alleyways I skirt around trickles of paint and water that are being washed toward a drain after an accidental spill or when they are washing out a vat after a batch has been mixed. The walls of the warehouse buildings and the alleyways and yards are stacked with barrels that contain the ingredients they use to concoct the paint. They seem to be scattered about randomly, but I know they must be organized by someone who can ensure that volatile ones are not close to each other in case of leaks. I am told that if I smell or see something out of the ordinary, report it. With all the peculiar sights and smells I encounter, I never think of any one thing being so strange as to bear mentioning. It never occurs to me that any of the volatile drums being rolled about could drop and spark setting off a huge explosion and immolating us all. These people know how to handle things safely and know what they are doing. Sure, like I know what I am doing.

Chapter 12

Downtown Louisville is a great place to be. It is several times larger than Lexington's downtown that heretofore I have regarded with wonder. I think Louisville must rival New York's Broadway. We don't have the tall buildings, but down at street level every inch of the sidewalk is crowded with ten-cent stores, clothing stores, record stores, movie houses, drug stores, restaurants, and bars. Everyone in town comes down here for their clothing, housewares, appliances, and entertainment. Neighborhood stores are mainly restricted to groceries, laundries, and mom/pop diners.

Between the river and Broadway it is a seething two-way flow of humanity on the sidewalks and crawling, raucous vehicles on the street. Parking is at a premium. No one ever seems to give up a hard-won space on Fourth. City buses patiently ply along depositing passengers at the corners when the drivers can get to the restricted spaces. And then bulling back into the traffic flow. Some drivers give up and go to one of the pay lots on the side streets or over on Third or Sixth. Out-of-towners staying at the Seelbach at Fourth and Walnut look down in wonder from their rooms at the spectacle or come out the door of the staid old hotel to join in the pageant.

There are people waiting for seats at the soda fountains of the Taylor and Walgreen drug stores, and the Woolworth and Kresges ten-cent stores. People stop at the Orange Julius and buy an orange juice and hot dog and eat them on the street. It is mad to even think about waiting for a table in one of the restaurants. Music from the department stores and record stores wafts out into the street. People gather in front of appliance stores to watch television and speculate on whether or not they can achieve such a clear picture in their family room. The salesmen assure them that they will get even better reception away from the interference of all these lights and power usage. They won't even need a chimney antenna since Louisville now has two television stations of its own with a third soon to begin airing.

There are lines queued up before the movie houses. They advertise their starting times and prices. They open at noon and run until midnight. The Brown Theater up by the hotel is the farthest from downtown. Then around the main area of Chestnut and Walnut are the Rialto, Palace, Mary Anderson, Loews, Kentucky, and Ohio. The latter two are not as grand as the others and play "B" pictures or old movies or westerns. There are supposed to be burlesque houses somewhere downtown, but I never see them. They must be tucked away on side streets or maybe farther down by the riverfront. I don't go down there looking. I wouldn't go into one of them anyhow. I would be embarrassed that someone from the plant would see me.

I can't help contrasting this place to Carlisle, the county seat where I have grown up. Carlisle has had a movie house off and on, but when it is open, it only has one showing a night. The few stores are in front of the courthouse square. All close by six o'clock, even on Saturday night. One or two restaurants stay open a couple hours longer. The drug store is open past nine as a service to people needing medicine and because the Greyhound bus stops there. But there has not been a late night bus through for years. The drug store light is like a lonely beacon. A solitary patrolman sits in the police cruiser across by the courthouse where he can watch the corner of Main and Broadway to catch imprudent motorists coming in from Flemingsburg who are too impatient to wait through the light to make their right turn and be on their way to Paris or Lexington. When we were courting, Juanita and

I joked at what a one-horse town it was and how the sidewalks rolled up at six o'clock. Now that I am here in Louisville, I think again how provincial it is and think about most of my classmates who are still there. I am sure that I can never go back and have no desire to except to see my mother.

In the fall of the year we are going to school. The old school bus runs out the Dogwalk Pike where the bushes and weeds grow into the gravel road. The school bus can barely squeeze through and when we meet another vehicle, both have to cautiously move onto the weedy shoulder and sometimes one has to back up.

We meet two trucks going back toward Morning Glory. We luckily have room to get by. The trucks pull off as far as they can and let us slip past. The trucks have wooden benches in the back and arched standards show where canvas covers can be placed in inclement weather. But the canvas is off today. The trucks are filled with German prisoners of war. They are being taken to work on one of the farms in the area.

We look each other over. We are too surprised to think up any catcalls or abuse to shout at them. Their war is over. They are being given the opportunity to work outdoors and get some sunshine. The farmers feed them, so they also get a little change in their food. They seem mildly curious, but they are a defeated bunch. They are unguarded in the back of the trucks. They could just jump off and disappear into the overgrown fields.

At school we talk about what we have seen. Very few of the farmers around ask for prisoner help. It must be someone who is late getting his crop in and is afraid the frost will get his tobacco. Can they really think of giving them tobacco knives that they will need to cut tobacco? The kids from Saltwell know of a family that contracted for prisoners to help them. They say that the woman offered them baloney sandwiches for lunch and they were grateful for them.

They are from another culture and must be bewildered by the tasks of growing tobacco. Ours must seem a strange and complex land. Can they even know where they are amid the warren of rough roads and overgrown farms? If any are of a mind to escape, they must quail at the thought of plunging into this wilderness. How would they survive? How would they ever hope to find their way back home? We see a movie entitled Escape in the Desert *about a bunch of Nazi prisoners escaping somewhere out west and terrorizing some people that own a store or gas station. It is a good action movie, but the actors seem more motivated than the prisoners we have seen on the trucks.*

With Juanita away I amuse myself by going to the movies a lot. On the farm I never got my fill of them. On Saturdays when we went to town they played the poorest movies or those they thought would appeal to children. We had a steady diet of Dead End Kids and Michael Shayne and Boston Blackie. We had serials that had started out sparkling with Spy Smasher and Nyoka of the Jungle and had dropped off to The Crimson Horseman and Superman in an ill-fitting costume. Westerns had similarly declined. The best movies were shown on Sunday or during the week, but we seldom got to see any of those. In Louisville I get my fill of this entertainment.

Soon after I arrive the Rialto advertises its new giant screen. I am doubtful that this will be any sort of good innovation that will enhance my enjoyment of movies. After all, I have seen 3-D and Cinecolor. But the giant screen does blow me away. I take to it right away. I have always watched movies on the little screen in Paris or at the old Bourbon Theater, or on television. Sometimes even at school where we had set up a miniscule screen. The Rialto has installed a screen fifty feet wide and as high as the ceiling will permit. I see a movie called *Fair Wind to Java* about the explosion of Krakatoa. The picture is grainy. I have to back away to take it all in. My head swivels back and forth to watch the action. I am sold on big screen viewing when I leave. The next week I am back to see Marilyn Monroe in *Gentlemen Prefer Blondes*. Marilyn is the icon of our generation. Her thirty-foot likeness is thrilling. I stay for a second showing.

Pretty soon all the theaters are installing big screens if they can fit them in. I stop in the drug store or dime store to buy some candy. And I treat myself to some movie popcorn. It has gone up to fifteen cents a bag. The prices are ridiculous. But I get my money's worth out of the fifty-cent admission fee. I typically sit through good movies two or three times. They are my Saturday and Sunday afternoon entertainment when I am in town. During the week I have to decide if the movie is worth staying out late to see multiple times if I am going to have to get up and go to work in the morning.

That summer I see *Stalag 17* and the science-fiction movie *War of the Worlds* at the Rialto. I go to the Loews and look at the ceiling that has hundreds of tiny lights set in a navy blue background simulating a night sky. I see *From Here to Eternity* numerous times. It seems that movies are better than ever. A controversy has sprung up over the content of *The Moon is Blue*. I go to see it but cannot see what the fuss is about. The discussion of sex and marriage on the screen is Hollywood's late attempt to throw off the strict censorship of the thirties and forties and have adult conversations between the principals.

One evening I attend a movie where a sneak preview is advertised. I forget about it and when the movie comes on it appears to be some kind of movie news. I am almost out of the theater when I see that it is a device and it is really the beginning of a movie. The young star is gorgeous in a gamin sort of way. I am enthralled by her. It is a sneak preview, and I cannot stay for a second showing. I am asked to fill out a card in the lobby with my remarks on the movie. I am lavish in my praise of the young star, Audrey Hepburn, and the movie *Roman Holiday*.

I see a western in 3-D called *Charge at Feather River*. The movie is pedestrian, but I love Max Steiner's score. I leave the movie humming the theme song. I see Clifton Webb in *Titanic* at the Brown Theater, and go to the old Kentucky Theater to see *Green Hell*. There is a horrible 3-D science-fiction movie called *Tarantula* with giant spiders and a show about giant ants called *Them*. An atomic bomb is about to go off and blow up people in *Split Second*.

When Juanita left Louisville, we have seen in the paper that a movie called *Bandwagon* will be coming around in mid-summer. We agree that we will see it and when they are playing "Dancing in the Dark," we will be thinking of each other. One Saturday when it is playing, I go to see it at the Loews. It is on with a Denice Darcel stinker about India. To see *Bandwagon* I have to sit through *Flame of Calcutta*. I watch *Bandwagon* three times and have to endure *Flame of Calcutta* twice. I watch "Dancing in the Dark" and think of Juanita thinking of me. Later I ask her if she has gone and seen the movie. She has but she doesn't remember our pact. We only had a one-way flow of vibes from the movie. Of Juanita and me, I am the romantic.

Mom sends another note to school to my fifth grade teacher, Miss Robbie. I don't know what is in the note, but Mom has told her of my illness and the importance of keeping me quiet and not having me romp around the playground or get into confrontations with my classmates. Miss Robbie sends me out of the room on a bogus errand and talks to my classmates while I am gone. She tells them of my illness and enters into a conspiracy with them to watch out for my well-being on the playground. When I come back from my errand, everyone in the class turns to look at me. I don't know what is up. Nobody will tell me. They just look at me knowingly.

I am suddenly very popular in the class. Miss Robbie seems to like me very much and value my opinions. My classmates do not seem envious. They don't call me teacher's pet. Girls and boys alike are friendly. My problem is at games. I know I am not permitted to run and tire myself out. But I still get around the farm and am sturdy. The little bit of running I would do on the playground is as nothing to what Jim and I do at home.

Still, Miss Robbie is watching over me and decides what games I can participate in and whether or not I am even allowed to go outside. She sometimes asks me to help do things such as clap the dust out of the erasers rather than play basketball, which I love, or participate in a game of tag. She stops the class from playing tag. It is the only way she can keep me out of it without making me an exception.

Virgil Howard is an older boy in our class. He lives far back in a hollow and his family only sends him to school a few weeks during the year. That is probably because the truant officer gets after his family. He has slowly made his way up to fifth grade. He reads at about a second grade level and can barely write. Arithmetic is a complete mystery to him. He is in school for a few days before the real cold weather sets in. He has not been in class when Miss Robbie told the class about my sickness and the need to watch out for me.

On the playground we have a disagreement. Virgil is not impressed by his snot-nosed classmate who can do no wrong in Miss Robbie's eyes. I am not backing off from this big caloot. We get into a shoving match. Virgil can shove harder. Others in my class try to intervene. Somebody says that Miss Robbie is calling us in and we break it up and go back to class looking daggers at each other.

Miss Robbie is surprised to see us troop back in before recess is over. Some clever girl had fabricated the call back just to break up our minor scuffle. Miss Robbie listens aghast as she is told by my classmates about my confrontation with Virgil. I stay silent. I am not a snitch. She forgets herself. She turns purple. She rails at him. She says that she has warned him that this was not to happen. She forgets that he was not at school that day of the note. If she told him later, he has probably just forgotten. She pulls him out of the seat and shakes him. She wants to slap him. I have never seen her so close to losing control. I am expecting the same treatment myself. Usually both participants in a fight are punished. When I see I am not to be punished, I try to say a few good words for Virgil. I can't see that he is so entirely at fault as to deserve this harsh treatment.

Miss Robbie takes Virgil out of the room to the principal's office. I think they have a talk. When they come back, I am amazed that he stops by me and apologizes for his actions. I accept his apology. This whole affair has been very curious to me. He rides my school bus. He sits far away from me and watches me murderously. He drops out of class in the late fall and never comes back again.

I see the movie *Houdini* with Tony Curtis and Janet Leigh. I am fascinated by the escape artistry of Houdini. I stop in the library and read about him. He has been a big attraction around the country and the world in the early part of the century. He has even made films in Hollywood. He died from a ruptured appendix. He was fascinated by the spirit world and died on Halloween.

Of course, his escapes were planned and for the most part accomplished by means of rigged restraints and contraptions. He secreted keys or wires on his person and accomplished his escapes while hidden behind a curtain. But during his lifetime he made a study of locks and tumblers and he could open a great many locks just by manipulating them. He made it look easy in the movie.

Down the front corridor of our office building is the lair of Bertha Combs. Bertha is a squat hunched lady of forty. She dresses plainly and she has never heard of makeup or hair stylists. All the girls in the surrounding offices are friendly to her. She doesn't compete with them for any job other than the one she has and no one else wants. She has been at Jones-Dabney for years. She works in a vault where the office supplies are kept, counted, and doled out. Anyone needing tablets or pencils or envelops must present a signed slip from Mr. Gerlach or one of the other principals to get any of Bertha's supplies.

She arrives in the morning with the other workers. She spins the dial on the vault door and enters and takes up her position on a little backless stool. Every time I enter the vault, she is always sitting on the stool. She brings her lunch – a sandwich. If she has to leave the vault for any reason, she locks the vault. There is no problem with theft of supplies at Jones-Dabney.

I keep my mail pouch in the vault at night. I go in at morning to retrieve it after I have my mail sorted and am ready to start my runs about the plant. I greet Bertha and get a weak grunt of "hi" in return. I don't know if she is inarticulate or just shy. She is withdrawn as if she expects to be hit or scolded by everyone. But then "Miss Personality" wouldn't take such a job. I wonder if they ever lost her how they would replace her.

Strangely enough, in the afternoon Bertha doesn't close the vault when she leaves. It is my duty. I could put the mailbag in before she left, but there is always the chance that I will spoil some envelopes on the old metering machine and will have to go get replacements. So when I am ready to go, I drop the mail pouch inside the vault, douse the light, close the door, turn the handle, and spin the lock.

In the movie Houdini is fired from a job making safes because he locks himself in one and attempts to open it from the inside. I look at the tumblers inside the door of the vault. It seems like a simple mechanism. You would just have to turn the dial until the various internal rods and latches line up and allow the handle to turn. I can close the door, and I will have the advantage over Houdini that there is plenty of light and air in the vault.

Thinking of the air inside makes me sound the first note of caution. If I can't get it open for some reason, can I last until morning when Bertha opens the vault? And if I am found in the vault, won't I be fired from my job? I am still confident that I can open the vault without knowing the combination. But why entomb myself? I will try it out first just by locking it.

About everyone is gone. Just Aggie is at the switchboard. Bev has had to leave early for some reason. Aggie is covering for her. They are punching out on each other's timecard. The cleanup men are in another part of the building. No one will come along to interfere with me. It won't take me long. I take a deep breath and grasp the long handle and lock the door.

The door drops a bar down that ordinarily will hold it from the inside. Now it prevents the door from closing. I can spin the lock and watch the back of the mechanism and watch the tumblers moving. I know that you have to turn it several times to clear it. I try turning it both directions, but the tumblers don't seem to be affected. I try to move them by hand on the inside of the door. My initial confidence is shattered. I am not going to get the door unlocked. And the vault will have to stand open all night. The cleanup people and others who happen by will just be able to go in and help themselves. If I cannot get it to close, I am going to have to stay there all night and guard it.

I run back to the switchboard in a panic. Aggie is getting ready to leave.

"The vault door has jammed in the open position. Who is around here who can open it?"

Aggie is puzzled for a moment. She answers with a question, as I know she will. "How did it get jammed?"

"Someone must have walked by and pushed on the handle and closed it. Now it won't shut."

She thinks. "Well, there is Mr. Gerlach and Madelaine and probably Virginia. Once when Bertha couldn't get in during a snow Virginia opened it and got supplies for people."

"Do any of them live close enough by here that they could come back and open it?"

"I don't know. We'd have to look them up in the telephone book. Why would anyone want to lock the door?"

"I don't know. I guess it was an accident."

"What about Norm Snyder? He is probably still here."

"You think he'd know?"

"I'll try him." She goes back to the switchboard. She calls him and then the first thing that has gone right this afternoon happens. Norm does know the combination. He will come right down and open it.

Norm works with the salesmen upstairs. He follows up on things around the office for them while they are away. He often works late hours. Like everyone else, he punches a clock, but he is on a salary. It is a lesson to me that this young personable guy gets ahead by out-hustling the others around the office.

Norm is not curious about how it happened. He has the combination written down on a piece of paper.

"I hope this still works. They may have changed it since I wrote it down."

I hold my breath. If it works I am off the hook. Aggie has wandered down the hallway to check on us on her way out. Norm completes the combination and lifts the handle. I almost collapse in relief.

"There you are. Do you need to go in?"

"No. My bag is already in there. I was surprised to find it already locked. Must have been done accidentally by somebody."

Now I want him to be gone. I want them to not make a big thing of it. I don't want to be questioned about it anymore.

I go back to the switchboard room to get my mail together. Aggie and Norm are following along talking. She drops her voice. "I don't know why he would have closed the door like that."

I think to raise my voice in protest. But I have already said it. They must not believe me. If I protest too much maybe they will have even more suspicions. Aggie goes out and Norm passes on his way back to his office. I thank him again. I heave a sigh of relief. What made me think I could be Harry Houdini? What if they had come in tomorrow morning and found me locked in the vault? I shudder. I have had a close call.

* * *

Uncles and Aunts at Blue Licks on the occasion of Uncle Joe and Aunt Matt's 50th wedding anniversary, March 1950; Lora Gaunce, Joe Hughes, Mattie Hughes, Naomi Gaunce, Cornelius Roe, Nannie Roe, W.J. Roe

* * *

Chapter 13

I can't believe I have reached the edge of adulthood without knowing about homosexuals. It was never mentioned in my home or school. Not among the rough work hands who stayed at our house or my classmates who mused about everything. Of course, I was reclusive, so I might have missed it. Maybe it was a tribute to people who sheltered children from such things that I had not picked up a glimmering, not from all my conversations or from the hundreds of books I read out of the school library.

Apparently, the kids of big cities like Louisville know all about the subject. The guys at lunchtime add the subject to our everyday conversations as naturally as they discuss the Colonels games or gossip about the hot girls around the plant. I listen in but cannot contribute. My knowledge of homosexuals and their escapades is still being developed. Jimmy Andrews is my chief instructor.

Forrest, since he works with the fastidious and mincing Bob Carroll, comes in for an unmerciful kidding from Jimmy. The others go along with it and laugh. I pretend to follow it and smile. Forrest thinks I am in sympathy with him. Jimmy uses any excuse to visit the Personnel offices so he can report in on what Bob is wearing and what new perfume he is sporting. I think Bob is just clean and well turned out and wants to be inoffensive to his co-workers, but I must agree that he sometimes overdoes the cologne.

I worry about my own body odors around the plant. It is summer and humid and most of the offices do not have air conditioning. I am sweaty when I get to the Personnel building.

Bob Carroll is cool and fastidious. He smiles and talks to me. I wonder if he is turned on by my sweat and odor. I bathe everyday now that we are in the hot weather. On the farm I walked back to the creek on warm summer evenings and bathed in the pool beside the wagon road that led to the cornfield. At my lodgings on Ormsby Street it is easy just to step into the bathroom and run water into the porcelain bathtub and scrub. My towel hangs with the other tenants who use the bath. Flora washes out the bathtub everyday.

Bob is not Jimmy's only target. In Shipping he works for a man of a similar preference as Bob. Jimmy's story is that he is always evading his boss who wants to put the moves on him. He amuses us by relating his close calls and vigilance not to be caught in a private place with him. Jimmy entertains us by making himself the poor innocent in his stories. He makes it sound like Little Nell being pursued by Oilcan Harry. Forrest eventually catches on and goes along with the joke reporting on Bob's maneuvers around the office.

I am still puzzled. Why do homosexuals want to prey on innocent or unsuspecting people who do not share their sexual bent? Why don't Bob and Jimmy's boss form a liaison? Maybe they don't find each other attractive. According to Jimmy they want young men like Forrest or me. I would be a disappointing lover. I could never bring myself to kiss a man. Or do whatever else they did in their furtive couplings. Jimmy says they have secret bars where they meet and have secret ways of identifying each other. They keep their activities hidden. It is against the law in Kentucky. That's another thing. How could I have been ignorant of such a thing so long? Apparently, the subject has been debated in the legislature in Frankfort and penalties imposed to prevent such behavior. How could I not know of it?

Maybe it was like when the preacher came to the school to lecture the kids about sex and never mentioned the word. And the closest he came was to warn about what petting would lead to. When I asked someone exactly what petting was they said that it was kissing. And I couldn't believe that the preacher would think that he could talk boys and girls out of kissing. It had turned out that petting referred to amorous caresses or couples feeling each other up. There was plenty that that could lead to all right. The problem was that no one came right out and discussed things head on. They talked in code words. If I couldn't follow it as much as I read, then I am sure that their messages just bounced off less-informed kids.

When Perry marries Wynona, he has to move out. She is a nice girl and Mom would gladly take them in, but the little house at Hooktown has only two bedrooms. There is no question that they can stay with us. Perry stills helps with the farm work, but they take a house nearby and set up housekeeping and he drives over every morning in the old Ford getting there in time to help with the milking. He puts in long days on the farm and his new bride is left alone. Sometimes she comes over with him and sits and talks with Mom all day as she does her chores. Mom teaches her to cook Perry's favorite dishes.

Pop is introduced to a man who lives in Cynthiana. Mr. Poulter is a businessman, but he has had the chance to purchase a large farm at Miller Station. It has a lot of acreage and a big tobacco base. It has a main house and two tenant houses. But he doesn't plan to live there. He wants someone to take the main house and rent out the two tenant houses and raise a crop for him and perhaps run some cattle and hogs and do all this on shares. Pop has been pointed out to him as someone who is trustworthy and industrious and capable of overseeing such an enterprise.

Pop is weary of worrying over the fortunes of the little farm at Hooktown. It has been hard struggling with two crops when help is scarce because of the war. He can make a profit by selling the farm. And he will be out from under the burden and the risks if something goes wrong. He has not dared to run cattle or sheep in case a couple should die and plunge him into debt.

He accepts Poulter's offer and he and Perry are like kids again planning out what they will do on the new farm. Perry and Wynona will take one of the tenant houses and a man named Eli Westfall and his wife the other one. Perry and Eli will help with the main tobacco crop and have small ones of their own. They will help with the hay and corn and cattle and receive a small monthly wage. But the tobacco will provide them their real cash money.

It is not a big change for us kids. The house is larger than the one at Hooktown. It is on the other side of the county, but we still go to Headquarters school. On the day we move Perry goes with the truck of furniture. He leaves Wynona with us kids. He will come back soon and get us. The noon hour passes and he does not show. We have not been left anything to eat. We sit on the running board of Perry's car. Wynona finds a stale Powerhouse candy bar in the glove compartment and divides it four ways. In mid-afternoon the man that drove the truck drops Perry off. He is apologetic about not getting back sooner. He loads us kids in the backseat and we are off to see our new home.

For the rest of his days Pop tells everybody that the biggest mistake he made in his life was selling the Hooktown farm. He gets along all right with Poulter, but he always longs to be his own man.

There is no doubt that Jimmy Andrews is straight. He has plenty of the girls around the plant panting after him. It reinforces my cynical opinion that girls gravitate to the biggest rotters of the male species. He tells stories on all the girls. I soon decide that he makes most of this stuff up. He knows of all the office romances. No one can keep an affair secret from Jimmy. It is entertaining and I, who have gone with only one girl in my lifetime, find myself envying him his rakishness. His stories indicate that he has a line of girls waiting to hop into his bed.

He still lives at home and has a next door neighbor who has her eye on him. She takes him into her basement and puts on a hula outfit and dances for him. She wants him in bed, but he demurs. She is only sixteen, he says. I can see that he is a young man of integrity. He tells of old romances during his days in high school. He gets the others to tell of some of their first encounters with girls. I keep my mouth shut. They are giving Jimmy plenty of ammunition to kid them later. When he asks me, I think first to say that I have not dated in high school, but I see that that will bring me in for a pounding. I say that my first dates have been pretty uneventful. I could tell them plenty. But I am learning to keep things to myself. Watch, listen, and learn and keep my mouth shut. You never learn anything when you are the one doing the talking.

But it is clear that Bob and Jimmy's boss are anomalies. Otherwise the world in Louisville is spinning just as it does in Nicholas County and love between men and women is what makes it go around. Everywhere on the streets I walk are courting couples. On the tennis courts young men and women play mixed doubles. In the movie houses they seek the dark corners to neck. Here, as elsewhere, they meet and date and marry. They meet each other's families and come to an accommodation with them. They find living quarters and acquire furniture and set about raising children who will be the next generation and continue the cavalcade.

I wonder how they meet and are sure that the mate they select is the right one. The songs say that for every man is a woman and you must search to find the right one. Some say it is preordained that you will meet up with the spouse that God intends for you to marry. I am not so certain. How can you be sure that out of the millions of girls in the world of near your own age you find the right one here in this little corner of Kentucky? If the GI's had not gone off to war, how would they have found the German and English and Japanese brides that they married and brought back with them? Divorce is still rare, but what happens if after you marry you find it was all a mistake and the one that was intended for you suddenly comes into your life. Maybe that was what all the great literature and better movies was about. The quest to find your true love and the consequences of mistaking an infatuation for the real thing.

My own expectations are that I will find some pliant and reticent girl like myself. Quiet and a reader. We will like to walk holding hands and look at nature. We will comment only to call the other's attention to some happening that might otherwise be missed. We will sleep late on weekends and listen to the radio and drift away. Maybe one will prop up on a pillow and read waiting for the other to come out of their drowse. Maybe we will make love and envelop each other in our arms and drift off to sleep again. I am not sure yet if Juanita is that girl, but I am sure that I will not find, nor do I want to, a girl like Jimmy's in the hula skirt.

When Clyde comes home from the South Pacific, he cannot give us any notice ahead of time. He has rotated out of his unit on Luzon where they have been preparing for the invasion of Iwo Jima. The soldiers have been out of the states since before Pearl Harbor with no extended leave and no way to visit home. He hits San Francisco and makes a long distance call to Aunt Eliza in Paris to let us know he is coming. Aunt Eliza calls down to our neighbor across the road who has a telephone.

We are in the back field behind a long ridge, where we cannot see the house, plowing and preparing the field for the planting of the tobacco plants that are growing now in their warm beds under the white tobacco canvas. We hear the dinner bell ringing and we know that something has happened. We start for the house, but some strange atmospheric phenomenon has caused the sound to reach us late. We have barely climbed the fence when we see Mom at the top of the ridge hurrying toward us. We wonder what could have happened. Pop and Perry must wonder if something has happened to one of the boys.

Mom is not used to running. When Pop reaches her she gasps out her story that Clyde is in San Francisco and will be back in two days. She is crying from happiness and she and Pop walk back to the house leaving Perry and Jim and me to unhitch and bring in the horses. Mom and Pop are beaming all evening. We can't wait to get to school next day and tell our classmates.

On the day Clyde comes back we beg Pop to let us stay home from school and go with him and Mom to Paris. He is reluctant, but finally gives in. We dress in the clothes we usually wear to town on Saturday. When we walk into Aunt Eliza's house on Railroad Street, Clyde is standing at a mirror in the kitchen in his uniform tying his necktie. Mom grabs him and hugs and kisses him over and over. Pop reaches to the side and shakes his hand again and again. We kids stand back and take it all in. The man before us is a stranger reddened by tropical sun and toughened by four years of war.

Clyde and my parents talk and Clyde tells about his journey and Aunt Eliza tells how he has appeared at her door the night before having made a connection to arrive on the late night train rather than the early morning one. Finally, he notices us kids and comes over and shakes each of our hands. He has a leftover candy bar and gives it to us. It is like a Mallo Cup and Jimmy divides it into three parts. I have never had one before and think it is one of the best things I have ever eaten.

When we get back to the farm, Pop sends Jim and me to help Perry who is weeding the tobacco beds. It is some time before they appear and Clyde is dressed in some of the old clothes he wore before the war. He and Perry have a glad reunion. Things are going to get back to normal now. The war will soon be over. But Clyde tells us his rotation is only for a month. Then he will have to report back.

Next day we take him down to see Aunt Naomi and on to see Aunt Matt. We kids decide to stay home and go with them. When Pop finds out, he chews us out good. We are not to skip any more school over this. We feel like we have to make every minute with him count. He is our older brother and we have missed out on his kidding and joking and playing around with us.

When his rotation is up, he does not return to the Pacific. He goes to Miami and is put up in a hotel for a while. He writes and tells us about his nights on the town and dancing with a WAC. It doesn't sound like Clyde. The war in Europe is winding down. The last battles of the Pacific are being fought. A system of points is formulated whereby men with many months of service and family obligations are released. Clyde has enough points to get out. So does Odell.

Clyde has brought back a bad case of malaria. When it strikes, he has to go to bed and Mom piles covers on him in the summertime and he shivers and sweats. We are baling hay with an old-fashioned stationary baler and Clyde has an attack of malaria and passes out and falls into the belt driving the baler. He breaks his jaw, which has to be wired shut. He has to live on soup and food that can be liquefied and ice cream. Mom and Pop won't let us kids have any of his ice cream.

One Sunday afternoon in the summer we are playing in the yard. A strange car pulls into the barnlot and four people get out. They stroll through the yard toward the house. A young man stops and shakes my hand. I am puzzled and it doesn't occur to me until he moves on that it is Odell with his wife and her parents come from Lexington to see us. I follow them slowly. They knock at the backdoor which is the custom and it is only a second until I hear the cry go up and Mom is hugging and kissing her first-born. We have got them both back safely from the war. But I see that we have all changed and it will not be the same for us as before.

I go into a movie one evening and find a good seat where I have an unobstructed view of the screen. There are a number of people in the movie, but enough empty seats to allow me to sit off alone. I have been watching the movie for a good while when a guy comes in and sits beside me. I am annoyed. There are plenty of empty seats around. He doesn't have to crowd me. I am paying little attention to him when I feel him jiggling his leg as though he is anxious or working off nervous energy. In a moment his leg is against mine still jiggling. I move away, and he moves his leg back against me. Now I am getting mad. I look at him and find that he is turned in his seat and looking fully at me. He is brushing his leg against me to get my attention. He motions with his head as though beckoning that I should follow him back to the restroom or outside. I am trapped between him and the wall at the end of the seats. I ask to be excused and push out past him. His hand brushes my fanny as I pass. I am not going to leave the theater. I have paid my money and want to see the movie. If he continues to annoy me, I will go tell the usher and have the fellow ejected. What would I tell him? I think. I go to another seat remote from my admirer. I see him still sitting where I have vacated. He doesn't seem interested in the movie. He looks over the crowd. And looks at me and I pretend to not notice him. After a while he gets up and leaves the theater.

I watch the movie twice and as I come out onto the streets the city seems to be shutting down putting itself to sleep. Doors have been closed and latched. In front of some, security gates have been accordioned across and secured by padlocks. But it feels like someone – maybe the street itself – is watching my slow passage back to my quarters.

Beyond the glitter and shine I know that back in the dark recesses of the city strange and lewd rituals are being enacted. Men and women sinning against God's word, in squalid and hidden venues, sating their perverse needs. Lusting for innocent and virgin flesh.

What went on was evil. But it could be seductive. I thought of silk stockings and green perfume. This could only happen – could only be found here in the nocturnal recesses of this city. The carnal, unspeakable, debauched city. This commerce of flesh – female and male so I have lately discovered. The ancient trade of vice.

A man stands at the corner eyeing the late passers-by. He sizes up who is on the prowl. He mistakes me for one looking for these sorts of pleasures.

"How about it, Buddy?" He moves in confidentially. "Want to see some girls?"

"No, thanks." I shake off the hand he has placed on my arm.

"Whatsamatter? No sense looking out here on the main street."

"I'm not looking."

"Everybody's looking. We got girls at the theater down on the next corner. Two dollars will get you in. They take off as much as the law allows."

"That right? And how much is that?"

"More than your innocent little eyes have seen before."

"I don't think so."

He follows me as I turn away. "So have you been out at night before? These girls – you know I can fix you up for a couple more dollars."

I don't want to get knocked in the head and have my billfold taken. The street looks dark except there is some kind of neon down a block or so.

I walk away shaking my head.

"Go on home to Mama," he says disgustedly.

I move along the nearly deserted street. At Broadway the movie at the Brown Theater is just letting out. People swarm around me. Their eyes are alight from the feature they have just attended. They chat about it. They are ebullient and anxious to be off to a late dinner, or to a nightcap at the closest bar, or to bed. I am back among the people I know. My step quickens for the walk home.

In the dark I lie in a luxury of clean sheets and downy pillows. I listen to the sounds of darkness – to crickets, a distant train, an occasional automobile, an orphan bird seeking a companion, a dog sounding an alarm. It is as much as the city ever sleeps. And time, forever flowing, like the Ohio only a mile or two away, moves me toward my predestined fate. And amid the fragrance of honeysuckle, and magnolia, and pine – I sleep.

It is a year since my bout of Rheumatic Fever and Pop judges that I am okay and can take on more of the work around the farm. He thinks the work is not so strenuous as the games Jim and I get involved in. Clyde is back from the army and helping out in the crop along with Perry and Eli so there isn't all that much for us kids to do. We have helped weed the tobacco beds and are hoeing the weeds in the tobacco and corn. Jim's place on the tobacco setter has been taken over by Clyde.

Perry and Eli's patches of tobacco are adjacent to the main crop in the same field. They know where one patch stops off and the other begins. When Pop runs the cultivator through his own rows he does Perry's and Eli's too. They have worked out a complex arrangement about sharing work. But Eli and Perry do their own hoeing and plow their own patches with the five-shovel.

Eli's house is below the barnlot just in front of our big house. His wife is always up at our place. She has a new infant and suckles him at her breast. It embarrasses us boys. They keep their windows and doors open at night and we can hear their loud talk and arguments. After supper, Eli brings the potato peelings out and plants them in his garden. He won't buy seed potatoes. Pop is doubtful that he will get much of a growth off the potato peelings.

Perry and Wynona's house is farther away up a long ridge. We go over there sometimes. They are happy, as two newlyweds should be. They have gotten some furniture but not near enough to fill the little house. They don't want to get into debt right off. Wynona seems like she should be in school or something. She plays with us kids. We are crazy about her.

Eli tells Pop that Perry has not honored some agreement about sharing the work. Pop takes it up with Perry. Perry says that Eli is lying. Pop sides with Eli. Perry loses his temper. He is going to go down and beat it out of Eli. Pop physically restrains him. Perry is bitterly disappointed that Pop will not support him in the dispute. They are both too proud and let the matter fester. We cannot believe it when Perry says that he is leaving.

He has been with us for eight years. He has been more of a big brother to me that my real brothers who have been away to war for half that time. He and Pop work out an agreement for Pop to pay him for the crop that is now half along. We think that he and Wynona will move somewhere close and that Pop and Perry will heal their dispute as they have in the past. But they move out of the county. We don't see them again until they come to Pop's funeral. And after that we become reconciled with them.

Chapter 14

The four girls in the main office are really the Accounts Receivable and Accounts Payable section of Jones-Dabney. They intercept the checks coming into the company and see that they are deposited. They handle cash disbursements that have to have Mr. Gerlach's signature on them. These are for all manner of purchases of raw material for the paint, drums and buckets that have been pre-ordered and are shipped to us, and office supplies. There is a special Payroll section that sees that the workers are paid.

Business is good at Jones-Dabney, and the girls are kept busy. Although they process the incoming checks, we have a large Accounting section that keeps track of all this, and receipts and correspondence is carried by me back to them. I stop by the main office at the start of each of my mail runs to pick up the incoming material that will be processed by Accounting and some of the other offices that day and maybe for several days to come.

The girls treat me like a little brother. Nancy Higgins is a born flirt. She kids the pants off me to get my reaction. They have found out that I have a girlfriend. They cannot imagine what she is like. I am so shy that they wonder how I ever got the nerve to ask her out.

"Woodie, what are you doing nights now that your girlfriend is gone?" she asks.

I don't have an answer ready. I know that whatever I say she will turn it into a joke. I am stuffing papers into my mailbag. "You know, eating out and going to the movies sometimes."

"Are you out looking for a new squeeze?" The other girls titter. I don't know what squeeze means, but I infer she means a new girlfriend.

"I am not looking, but am always open to new opportunities." I am prepared to exchange jibes with her.

"How about all the girls here at Jones-Dabney? Why don't you give some of these girls a chance?"

I know she is joshing me. She and Virginia are only a couple years older than I am, but they are many years older in sophistication. As a boy just off the farm I wouldn't have the nerve to approach them.

"I don't know much about any of the girls here. What if I went to one to ask for a date and made the mistake of hitting on somebody that was already married?"

That brings more laugher from the others, but Nancy keeps a straight face. "You can't be put off by that. They'll straighten you out if you make a mistake. Besides, maybe you'll hit on a married girl that wants a little strange into her life."

"What?" Is she calling me strange?

"You know, I mean someone different."

"Oh. No, I hope to get back with my girl."

"When are you going to see her again? Christmas?"

"No. I hope before then. She might drive in with some people from her work and spend a weekend here."

"So you are planning a wild weekend at your place?"

"Oh, no. We have some friends in town. She would stay over there." I don't want them to misunderstand.

"Woodie, you are hopeless," she concludes.

"I guess."

"You are a good kid." I smile at the compliment. I have filed the mail. I am off to make my mail run. "The trouble is, who likes good kids?"

I blush and their laughter follows me down the hallway.

Sherman is a mechanical tinkerer. He is always trading cars and constantly under the hoods putting on a new water pump or replacing spark plugs or something. He and Geneva and their first-born, Linda, live in Norwood, a Cincinnati suburb, and he works at one of the auto plants. He has got on there before all the other guys returned from the war. Pop dotes on his new granddaughter and we look forward to their visits to the farm about every other weekend.

Sherman is an old farmboy from Southern Kentucky. He has been in the Navy and his ship was sunk out from under him. Swimming away in the burning oil he inhaled fire and damaged his lungs. He is released from the Navy before the end of the war and meets Geneva and they fall in love, and she divorces her first husband to marry Sherman. He is making good money and they have a nice apartment. Later they will have television long before we get one, and Sherman takes these apart as well to see how they work and how to fix them. Like I say, he is a born tinkerer but a lot of fun to have around.

They come to the farm and he is driving a huge car – a Graham – that he has traded up to. It is a powerful car and can eat up the miles between Cincinnati and the farm. He raises the hood and proudly shows off the engine to my brothers and cousins who are visiting. Gas is still under twenty cents a gallon but that seems a lot in these days.

They come to the farm on Saturday morning and have to return Sunday night. It is wrenching for me every time they have to leave. It is as if they have lighted a network of neon about us and it is extinguished each time they leave. Mom gives Geneva eggs and butter and gives her granddaughter a hug and there are warm goodbyes for they will be back in a couple of weeks.

But it is more than I can bear. I silently pray. Don't go. Don't let them go. I can't stand it if they go.

I watch them pull away and wave with the others. I am desolate. They are going. They turn out the gate and start up the hill away from Miller Station. There is a mild pop. The Graham stops on the hill.

It slowly backs to the gate. We run down there. Have they forgotten something? Sherman is out and looking under the car. He doesn't diagnose it at once, but he has a broken axle.

They cannot get back to Norwood. We go harness the horses and pull the Graham up in the barnlot where Sherman can work on it under a shade tree. The next day Geneva calls to the plant in Cincinnati and tells them of the problem. They will hold Sherman's job. At the garage in town they will have to order the axle. There are not many Grahams on the road. Sherman wishes he were in Cincinnati. He could go to a junkyard and get a replacement.

They have to stay with us for a month while the car is being repaired. Geneva is frantic that Sherman will lose his job. I feel guilty that my prayer has kept them here. It is the first time I have had something like that answered. Although it is wonderful to have them living with us, I see that it has caused them difficulties. I will have to be careful in the future.

Joan Overmire is one of the two married Joans in the front office. She is a pretty blond. She has gotten backed up on her work and must stay late to finish up. This causes her to miss her ride. Her husband will stop by to pick her up at about the same time as I will be finishing for the day.

Bev is staying late at the switchboard, and we make small talk as we always do while I am getting the last package of mail for the day ready to go out. I have to see that it is in the mailbox a block away for a 6:10 pickup. I usually leave at six o'clock and stroll over to the mailbox and go on home from there. Sometimes I could finish well before that, but I need the overtime money, so I don't make any great effort to leave any sooner.

The calls drop off after five o'clock and there is not much for Bev to do either. She talks a little about her husband who has big plans but can't seem to get a job to match his huge talent. He has had a couple jobs but quit them when he found that the work didn't meet his expectations. It still sounds to me like they are sponging off Aggie, although it is clear that she likes her daughter living with her.

At 5:30 Bev has gathered her things and is ready to depart. She wishes me a good night and punches out on the time clock in the entrance hall. I continue to meter the mail and glance over at Joan who is busy at her desk. Two of the colored cleanup men come by. When they see her in the office they dump the trashcans and leave to do other parts of the building. I have only a nodding acquaintance with them.

I finish for the day and prepare to leave. Joan comes from her desk to stop me.

"Woodie, can you stay with me until my husband comes?"

"I have to get the mail posted."

"What time do you have to go?"

"Six o'clock at the latest. I have to have it in the box for the pickup."

"I'm afraid to stay alone with the cleaners."

I hadn't considered that. I could see how she might be afraid. I am in a quandary.

"Are you ready to punch out?" I ask.

"Yes, but I can't stand outside in the rain."

"I tell you what. Let's get punched out and I'll take the mail to the box and then come back to stay with you until your husband comes."

"Oh, would you? I'd be so grateful. I know I'm a fraidy cat, but those men really scare me."

"Just stand there in the doorway and hold it open. I'll watch all the way to the mailbox and back."

There are lights on each side of the door. They are always on and a night guard is around somewhere. But he must patrol the entire plant. He has a key and punches in at several time boxes to show that he has made his rounds on schedule.

Joan is framed against the door, holding it ajar. I hurry to the mailbox. She is beautiful and petite. I hope she is married to a sturdy guy. One who respects her and can protect her. I had not before thought of how it must be a frightening world to some people like Joan who have to be on guard constantly to not get themselves in a position where they might be molested. I hurry back to the office, but I feel inadequate to protect her.

We stand just inside the doorway looking out. She is fretful that her husband is late and apologetic that she is keeping me from leaving. I have nothing planned except to go out to the drugstore and buy my supper. Perhaps in the rain I will go around to Tony's which is much closer to my room. I have not brought an umbrella to Louisville with me.

At last Mr. Overmire pulls up in a late model car. He and Joan are already doing well holding two jobs and postponing starting a family. I say goodnight and start to walk off, but Joan won't hear of it. They are going down Hill Street and will drop me by the house. I don't want them going out of their way, but accept a ride to St. James Court where I will cut through the park and back to my house.

After their first exchange of greetings Joan voices her pique at his lateness. Then quickly it is brushed aside and they are speaking of matters relating to their home life and things they have agreed to get done that day. I am quite forgotten in the backseat.

The farm at Miller Station is a large one and we have a large crop. Eli Westfall has part of it and we are growing our crop combined with Perry's. Pop puts another tenant in Perry's house to work for us by the month. His name is Sam Yazell. Mom complains that the family is trashy and she won't have anything to do with them. Yazell is rather old, but he has teenage children and some of them help in the tobacco. Juanita Yazell is a particularly attractive young girl and people say she will not be staying around much longer. The children do not go to school, and I don't know whether or not they can read and write.

Sam Yazell is always running his mouth and bragging and telling stories. I am old enough to have some doubt as to their authenticity. But they are entertaining and it helps us pass the time in the tobacco patch. He tells of paying fifty dollars to see one of Joe Louis's fights. He thinks it was a gyp. He has seen better fights in a bar, he says. He tells about the various towns he has lived in all over the country and says he always carried a large western style revolver on the seat in his car. He has shot it out on a couple of occasions. He still carries a bullet just under the skin of one leg. In case we have any doubts, he rolls up his pants leg and lets us feel the slug.

He says that he has been in the Spanish-American War. That would make him older than my father. He says that he was there in camp that morning and saw Teddy Roosevelt and the Rough Riders move out to attack San Juan Hill. He heard the fight in the distance and saw them ride back into camp that evening. He makes it sound like the troops came back tired from the effort rather than elated over their success. It sounds like a true story.

Yazell takes the money he and his family earn during the month and moves on. He is not the kind to put down roots anywhere. He probably will go back to bootlegging. Pop is always afraid that they will steal something while they are with us. He doesn't put another tenant in the house that Perry had earlier occupied.

Virginia Gray is tall and slim with auburn hair. She is fair and freckled, which betrays her Scots-Irish ancestry. She has come to Louisville from the mountains to find a better life. I wonder if she visits back there. I think she has made an even more dramatic change in her life by coming to this city than I have. She hasn't a car and rooms with two other girls in an apartment on the corner of Hill and St. James.

She works late one afternoon and asks to walk along with me on our way home. She is gloomy. Her boyfriend is Bruce Abell who works over in the R & D building. They have had a spat. I drop the mail off and we start to walk along the left sidewalk. She unburdens herself about Bruce.

"We had a date this evening, and he called it off without giving me a reason."

I am quiet. I can't give lovelorn advice.

"He treats me like dirt. I don't know why I stand for it."

I start to say, like father, like son. His father is the insufferable Walter.

"I don't have many friends here in Louisville. He and I have been going together for almost a year. Wouldn't you think that we would have some plans by now? But I have no idea of his intentions."

"He seems like a pretty nice guy. They pick me up once in a while at mornings when I am getting the mail."

"I think he is pretty nice too. That's why I go with him." She sighs soulfully. "Maybe I am too nice to him. But I guess he is grown used to it. Now he takes me for granted. He knows I'll be waiting. And he can choose to see me or leave me sitting in my room, like tonight."

"He has rocks in his head to leave you alone."

It has slipped out. I hadn't meant to say it. I think she is lovely, but older and a thousand feet above me. I hope she hasn't caught it, but she pauses and looks at me fondly.

"You're sweet, Woodie. I bet you never treat your little girl this way."

I never think of Juanita as a little girl. But, no, I have never stood Juanita up except once when I busted the oil pan on our car on a rock on Oxbow Hill Road coming over to see her.

"Well, sometimes something can come up that has to be taken care of," I say lamely, hoping to give her a way to rationalize her inconstant lover.

"Oh, poop. He just wanted to go to the ballgame or afternoon fishing, and he didn't even take the trouble to make up a good excuse. He just calls me at three o'clock and tells me that he isn't coming. It makes me furious. I did my hair last night and grocery shopped in case he wanted to eat in rather than take me out."

"That was thoughtful of you," I was noncommittal.

"And my roommates agreed to go out to a movie so we could have the place to ourselves."

We walk in silence for a while. I don't want to imagine Virginia making love to Bruce Abell in her bed in the apartment on the corner of Hill and St. James.

She is a sturdy walker. I wonder if she has lived on a farm or come from the town of Hazard itself. I think that it is coal-mining country. I am dying to ask if she knew of the feuds around there fifty years ago. None of that seems appropriate to bring up just now.

"Well, I'll get over it," she says determinedly. "Next time I see him we will get this straight between us. I'm not putting up with any more of his crap."

"Maybe it's just a big misunderstanding. Something important may have come up, and it was something that he didn't want to burden you with."

"We don't have to talk about it any more. Thanks for letting me unload it on you. You're a good listener."

"Anytime. It's swell walking along with you." It crosses my mind to wonder what she would say if I asked her to go out with me this evening to a movie or something to take her mind off her disappointment. I glance at her again. She is twenty or twenty-one. I am eighteen, but look younger. She would be embarrassed if I asked. I don't want to risk our friendship.

We are in front of her apartment house. I prepare to tell her good night and go on to my house.

"Woodie, I have all the food I bought to use up. Why don't you come in and let me cook you a good meal. I bet you always eat burgers and grilled cheese sandwiches."

"I couldn't let you do that." I am taken aback. "I bet Bruce will be over here tomorrow night, and you will still be able to cook it for him."

"He won't get a bite if he waits for me to cook it for him. No, I am cooking it tonight and what we can't eat I'll throw out in the garbage."

I still hesitate. This has happened too fast. "Your roommates and you can eat it."

"No. I told you that they won't be here. They have gone to a movie."

"Maybe you would like to go to a movie too and not have to be here tonight. We can walk over to Oak Street or ride the bus downtown."

She won't let me walk away. She takes my hands and tugs me toward the front door. She drops her voice.

"Don't you like me, Woodie? Don't you want to come in? Why should we be alone in our rooms tonight?"

"I like you a lot," I find my voice. Is this really happening? It is something out of a movie. "If you are sure you want to cook I'll come in."

The apartment is empty as she said it would be. She sits me in the parlor and turns on the television for me.

"I want to change into something else," she says. I expect that she wants to save her good clothes for the office and put on some more comfortable shoes, although she has walked all the way home in the ones she has on.

She leaves the door to her bedroom ajar and talks to me while she is changing. My thoughts are in turmoil. What would she do if I walked in there? What does she expect me to do? She has been disappointed by her boyfriend. Is she planning something foolish to get back at him?

The telephone rings. I start. She yells out that she will get it. She comes out of the bedroom hurriedly tying a robe about her. I have seen a glimpse of brassiere and panties. She has shed her hot slip.

She takes up the telephone and it is Bruce. My heart drops. I know that he has called to apologize. Amid my disappointment I am still amused to hear the tone she takes with him. The icy demeanor that she has shown all the way home has thawed and she talks to him in sugary loving terms.

I can tell from the one end of the conversation what is being said. He is sorry. He stills wants to keep their date. She hesitates. She looks at me. She starts to make an excuse that she is washing her hair. I get up and shake my head. I indicate that I am leaving. She shakes her head back to me and takes on a hurt look as though she doesn't want me to go. I know that she doesn't mean it. She wants Bruce to come on. I smile and wave her a goodbye. She asks Bruce to hold a minute. She presses the phone to her breasts.

"I'm sorry, Woodie," she whispers.

"It's okay," I whisper back. "Have fun. Make him beg."

"I will." She puckers and pantomimes a kiss to me. All the way home I ponder how those lips would have tasted.

We have raised Pete from a pup. He is some kind of mixed breed bird dog and he would have been good for hunting rabbits, but Clyde and Odell, who would have taught him, are in the army. He is not as clever as our previous dog, Tip, was. He goes with us to the field to drive in the cows, but he won't herd them. He is a good companion but of no help on the farm.

Our dogs do not come in the house. He has an old doghouse. He will not go into it except in the most extreme cold weather. We throw a couple old burlap sacks in there to keep him warm. On hot days when he is with us in the fields we sometimes see him go down to the creek and paddle around getting cool. We envy him. Jimmy and I cannot swim.

He eats scraps from our table. He is not overfed. We need most of our discarded food for the hog slop. We fatten hogs to kill in the winter. The family needs the meat to live on. The dog is not a necessary part of the farm. He is not pampered. His meal is often a cold biscuit.

We are at breakfast one morning just after Clyde has returned from the war. Four men and a bunch of dogs enter our yard. Pop meets them at the backdoor. They are rough looking men with shotguns and rifles and have been up all night. They have Pete on a rope. He has been caught running with a pack of dogs that have been killing sheep. There is no blood or wool on Pete's muzzle. But these men are adamant that he must be destroyed. They see us kids in the background. They know he is our pet. They move off a ways and talk to Pop. They leave Pete with him.

We are farm kids. We are attached to Pete but we know very well that a sheep-killing dog must be gotten rid of just as any other one that takes away a farmer's profit by killing chickens or sucking eggs. Dogs don't learn to kill on their own but by running in packs. We know that Pete is often gone most of the night coming in tired and laying around a good bit of the day.

When we get home from school we are told that Clyde has taken Pete out in the woods and shot him. We accept it though we feel bad about it. We find out a month or so later that Pop has not had the heart to do it knowing how much we kids like Pete. He has taken him down to Uncle Joe's and tied him up. He is hoping that staying down there for a while he will forget about the pack and stop his sheep-killing proclivities if he ever had any.

But he won't stay tied up. He howls at night and keeps Uncle Joe and Aunt Matt up. When they untie him he runs off. He is gone for a couple days and when he returns Uncle Joe ties him up in the barn.

When Pop goes to see about him, Uncle Joe tells him that he must take him back. The men have told Pop that if he is caught among their sheep again, they will bring legal action. Pop and Clyde have no option but to shoot him.

Pete is the last real family pet we have. Other strays come to our house. Most times we run them off. We let a few stay on. We keep a cat or two in the barn to kill mice. We are a farm family and are not sentimental about pets.

* * *

Juanita Caswell (1953)

* * *

Chapter 15

Washington and Louisville are separated by 600 miles. The most direct route is across old U.S. Route 50. Coming out of Washington it is a pretty good road through Virginia until you reach the West Virginia hills. The Alleghenies and the Blue Ridge and the Cumberlands throw up a north-south barrier and each mountain is encountered and surmounted by running up diagonally and crossing at the top, then similarly running angularly down the reverse side, swinging the wheel to cross the inevitable bridge at the bottom and repeating the process over and over. If you could drive as the crow flies, it would be much shorter. But the weary motorist must negotiate switchback after switchback to traverse the width of West Virginia.

He comes out of West Virginia finally, thankfully, at Parkersburg and happily settles into the run across southern Ohio. Here he can pass the big trailer trucks that stymied him on the narrow blind road in the mountains. If his brain is still working and not befogged by the strain of ten hours of the hardest kind of driving, he can make better time now. But fatigue will overtake him, particularly if he has driven the route overnight. It is a good time to have a relief driver so you can catch a quick nap hunched down in the passenger seat.

Across Ohio then to leave the National Highway and turn onto the road that runs down the river to Louisville. If you have left work the afternoon before and driven as hard as you could and with another driver spelling you a couple times, and only having to stop a few times for gasoline and food and potty breaks, you pull into Louisville soon after the sun rises. But on a Saturday morning the town is still asleep. You have normally busy streets all to yourself and you look forward to dropping off your passengers and getting a warm greeting and a hot breakfast at your parents' house.

On the farm we never pay any attention to Labor Day except that it is a bother to not get a paper that day since the mail carrier doesn't run. Now both Juanita and I have a three-day weekend. She has had the opportunity to join five other FBI employees and drive in for the holiday. They each contribute five dollars to the driver to pay for his gas and to give him a bit extra for the wear and tear on the car. It is a harrowing and tiring trip and they must go back on Monday. So it is only a very short stay. But Juanita comes to me.

She has not told her family. They would be hurt to find out that she came to Louisville rather than the farm. She and I will have the weekend together. Wilma Jo still does not have a telephone, so I just catch the bus and go on over there. Juanita has arrived a couple hours earlier and Wilma Jo says that she is sleeping now. I go in and she looks beautiful lying in bed dead asleep. She is in one of Wilma Jo's gowns and nestled under the covers that she and Carl have lately given up. In the single room she has no choice but to sleep under the observation of all the occupants. I don't think she would normally want to be sleeping in Carl's company.

But these are different times. We must take our time together as it is given to us. I sit and drink coffee with Wilma Jo and Carl and we talk quietly. There are only two kitchen chairs in the room and a little stuffed sofa. It is adequate for them but not good for entertaining company.

She finally stirs and smiles at me. She is drowsy and her hair is tousled. She is lovely. I have been lonely too long. I sit beside her on the bed. We kiss and she turns her head away. She wants to brush her teeth. She asks Carl and me to go outside while she dresses and takes care of her morning toilette. Carl and I walk around the block. When we come back Juanita has dressed and combed her hair. Wilma Jo is setting sweet rolls out on the table. We eat rolls and drink coffee. Juanita and I devour each other with our eyes. She must leave at noon on Monday. It seems like all the time in the world.

Soon after he returns from the Pacific, Odell and his wife, Midge, separate. He comes to stay with us. He is quiet and endures Pop's barbs and takes up his old life on the farm. He doesn't seem happy with us, but he is at loose ends right now. He takes the little horse-drawn mower and mows the horseweeds and ironweeds that have sprung up in the field across the creek. The back of the field is bordered by a rock fence that he will dismantle later that year when he chases a rabbit into it that he is trying to kill for our dinner table.

But now it is into September and we are just finishing tobacco housing, and we have started back to school. We come in one day and listen to the radio. It is news of the war. At school we have been talking about the atomic bombs that have been dropped on Japan. Some say they are as big as a small house and can barely be carried by the B-29's. They are devastating and we can wipe out entire Japanese cities with one of them. We have lost a lot of soldiers in the war and reports of Japanese atrocities have come back to us for four years. No one is in sympathy with the Japanese civilians. We hope for more bombs to be dropped.

But when we get in from school, the news is that the Japanese have surrendered and the war is over. I hate to tear myself away from the radio, but I have to take a bucket of water to Odell in the field. I find him doggedly mowing the little swatches that the short sickle on the mower can reach. I tell him about the surrender. He has spent four years fighting the Japs. He didn't think they would give up no matter how much you bombed them. He unhitches the horses and we

*ride them in from the field. I wonder if Pop will be mad at him for
quitting early.*

*He turns the horses out and comes to sit with us in the kitchen and
listen to the reports of the celebrations in New York and Washington
and San Francisco. The reporters are out on the street and you can hear
car horns blaring and snatches of impromptu songs. They interview
servicemen just back from Europe who are relieved that they will not
have to go to the Pacific. They interview parents who now know they
will get their sons back safely.*

*Pop and Clyde come in. They have been down at the farm that
Clyde has bought near Blue Licks with the money he made during the
war. They have been listening to the news on the car radio. We all
sit in the kitchen and listen to accounts coming in. Odell and Clyde
listen to everything. It is as though they can't believe it is all over.
Finally, Odell gets up and gathers the buckets to go do the milking.
The little chores of the farm cannot be put aside by the big events of
the world.*

Juanita could go to a hotel for a couple of nights, but Wilma
Jo has invited her to stay and sleep on the little sofa. A hotel room
would give us some blessed privacy, but we have to be realistic.
We need to save our money and the Watkins's offer is heartfelt.
It is nice to have good friends in the city. Besides, Wilma Jo and
Juanita have long been buddies, and they now have a chance to
catch up on all their gossip and fill each other in on the events
back on the farm.

Wilma Jo and Juanita's families live on farms that nearly adjoin,
but you have to go on up Taylor Creek Road and turn onto Oxbow
Road to get to Juanita's house. In school they sat together when
the teachers allowed it, and passed notes when they couldn't. They
copied each other's homework and talked about boys and groused
about their teachers and looked forward to the trip back home on
the school bus at the end of the scholastic day.

Wilma Jo's sister is my brother Odell's second wife. We have often been to their house. I know the Gaunces well just as Wilma Jo knows the Roes. Maybe that is unconsciously how Juanita first became attracted to me, hearing Wilma Jo talk about my brother or my family.

Her married sister has joined her mother and father decrying Wilma Jo's marriage to Carl. She has hoped to get Wilma Jo to leave Carl and come back to them on the farm. She has been vocal in the family discussions that resulted in the sheriff being notified and an investigation made in Louisville to try to find them. Later, Wilma Jo calls back home and after she is sure they are reconciled to her marriage, she gives them her address so they can correspond.

The first letter she receives from her married sister is a tirade directed mostly at Juanita. She is convinced that Juanita has schemed with Wilma Jo to cause her to run off with Carl. And she is convinced that it is Juanita who has brought them to Louisville and sheltered them and abetted them in their marriage. She still hopes to get Wilma Jo to come back. She lays all the blame on Juanita as a girl of low morals and a bad influence on Wilma Jo.

Wilma Jo lets Juanita read the letter from her sister. Juanita is outraged, as am I. The next time I see her, I am going to set her straight. If it should ever happen that Juanita and I married, we would have this idiocy on record to spoil the family's harmony. Juanita pretends to laugh it off, but later she vents her temper against my sister-in-law.

But that is all forgotten for now. We plan our day. We will get back to all our favorite places. We can ride the bus to downtown. We will stroll along Fourth Street and visit Central Park. We will stop at an Orange Julius and get a banana split at Taylor's Drug Store. Maybe we will even ride down to Iroquois Park. Wouldn't it be nice to stumble across a parade or a carnival? We will exult in each other's company. We will steal sweet kisses and fond caresses. And when dusk falls, we will find somewhere to be alone.

For anyone afraid of snakes, central Kentucky is a bad place to live. The limestone strata provide numerous chinks, crevices, and caves where they can live and lurk. Mice thrive in its fertile fields and feed the snakes. Snakes are a blessing to the farmer who needs their help to control the mice population, but are a terror to a child who is afraid of them. Most farmers are heedless of their virtues and kill them when they see them. Of course, there are poisonous ones among them — moccasins and copperheads. But I have never known anyone to die of their bites.

Aunt Mary Liz shows us the place on her leg where she was bitten by a viper in the yard of their house in Fleming County. It is blue around where the snake bit her and she says that her leg was swollen for several days, and she was in danger of losing it.

We kids are taught to fear snakes because we see the adults' reaction to them. Every time I see one of these encounters where it seems like a battle to the death with the snake, I have nightmares for days afterward. I lie in the bed at night and cover my head imagining that snakes are crawling in with Jimmy and me. My whimpering wakes Jimmy up. I tell him there are snakes on the bed. He sits up and runs his hands over the covers to show me all is well. Our talking has awakened Mom and Pop. They come with a lamp to see if one of us kids is sick. I am scolded and told to stop this nonsense. I am keeping everybody awake.

At Hooktown, and again at our place at Miller Station, we have creeks on our farms that are populated by water moccasins. We are warned to avoid them. As small children at Hooktown, we see them lying out in the water submerged with just their heads periscoped. We pick up flat shale rocks and skim them across the water trying to clip their heads off. At Miller Station I am walking barefoot back along the creek to find our milch cows. I step on a large moccasin. Too late

I sense the fetid smell. In a moment of adrenalin rush I broad jump away from him to set some kind of record for a kid my age. I take Odell back to kill it, but it has disappeared. The weeds are mashed down, and its smell lingers. I go back to wearing shoes.

In Bourbon County the snakes don't seem as populous. But we know they are there. We have water in the house, though Pop doesn't let us boys use the indoor bathroom. He thinks Mom and Colleen are wasteful of the water. We have both a well and a cistern. In the dry months of the summer the well dries up. We have to switch over to the cistern. We open it to add chemicals to the water — mainly chlorine to kill parasites that may be lurking. We see a large snake swimming in the water below. Obviously he has made its dark recesses his home and comes up at night to go out and hunt mice. There is nothing we can do about him. Pop throws in the chemicals and we close the top of the cistern. We are warned not to tell the women of the snake. We have no choice but to go ahead and use the cistern water, but it is a relief when we can switch back to the well.

Jimmy and I are walking along the railroad one day and find a snake stretched out across the tracks. We are afraid to pass it. We go back to the field where the men are baling straw left when we combined the wheat. One comes back with us and skewers the snake with his pitchfork. He takes it back to the others and pretends like he is going to put it on one of the colored men. The Negro tells him that if he touches him with that snake, he will go get a gun and kill him. He is serious. Some of the men try to laugh it off, but the joke has soured. The man goes on and kills the snake.

I mostly try to avoid encounters with snakes. But when they happen, I let someone else undertake the combat. Later when Jimmy gets his rifle, we can shoot them and it seems less a danger to stand off some feet away and blast away at them with a rifle. In Kentucky you mostly have to learn to live among them. They are everywhere. You are always watchful. You learn to walk looking at the ground beneath your feet. You don't reach blindly into dark places where one may be lurking. And you dread the day when you find a shed skin near the house that indicates that you are hosting one, or more likely two, since they are usually mated.

The town comes awake slowly on the holiday. Normally bustling Broadway has a desultory trickle of cars. Some people out going to picnic in a park, others invited to lunch with friends or family, some just driving to get out of the town for a while. We stand behind a transit bench until the bus passes by and then move up to sit and talk. No one is waiting for the bus this morning. This is the appointed place where Juanita will meet her ride for the trip back to Washington.

"Didn't you say two other people were going to show up here?"

"Yes, Roger lives down near Owensboro. He dropped us here on the way through and said for us to be here at noon."

"Well, it's still early."

"I don't want to take a chance on missing my ride. I would have to take the bus and it takes more than twenty hours. Besides, I have already paid him."

"That must be pretty uncomfortable with six of you crowded in there."

"Sitting on the side you can lean against the window and sleep some. There are four girls and Janice is his girlfriend so she rides up front in the middle. So we other three girls in the back take turns in the middle. Even then you get so sleepy that you nod off. Roger and Kenny get a nap now and then in the passenger seat. I am afraid one of them will go to sleep while they are driving."

I look at her fondly. She has gone to a lot of trouble to be with me this weekend. We have made the most of it. We have been up most of the two previous nights. I am going to turn in early tonight. She will have to nap when she can in the car and report to work a few hours after arriving back in D.C. But we are young and resilient. We will recover in a couple days.

"If you see my aunt and uncle in Paris, don't let it slip that I have been here."

"I won't. But I haven't seen them on any of my weekends back. Do they still go to town on Saturday?"

"I don't know. I don't think A.W. goes to the show much. He would rather stay home and watch television."

"Wait till he gets a girlfriend and he will be going up there often."

She smiles and nudges me playfully. "Oh, he won't have to meet his girlfriend in the movie. Uncle Jess will let him have the car whenever he wants it."

"When are they coming up to see you?"

"Next month. I'll have to show them around. They want to see the Capitol, the White House, and the Washington Monument."

It has only been just over a year since our Senior class was up there and we saw all those things. I would sure like to be going back up.

"I wish the FBI would contact me. Are you sure they are hiring on?"

"Yes, they are always asking that we give them names of people who might be interested in working up there. I can't understand why they haven't called you."

"Maybe they got the address wrong or something. Maybe you should tell them again."

"Maybe I will." She looks up at a girl hurrying down Broadway. She must have dropped off a city bus some blocks away. "Here comes Clarice now."

They meet in loud greeting and I realize that we can no longer talk privately and lovingly. After she is introduced to me, the two girls catch up on their weekend activities. They are anxious about the third girl they are to meet here.

"Roger said he couldn't wait. If she is not here, he is going on and she will have to fly or catch the bus."

I think that they would have more room in the car if that happened. But I don't say anything.

"Oh, here is Roger now," Clarice says, appalled that their friend may be left behind.

He sounds his horn and pulls into the space reserved for the bus. He comes around to open the trunk and take their little bags. A girl greets us from the front seat and a boy my age crawls out of the backseat to move up front. There is a short sharp exchange about the other girl not having arrived. Clarice pleads to give her another five minutes. Just then she arrives in another car pulling in behind them. They are on schedule.

While the last bags are being arranged and the last girl is saying goodbye to her mother, Juanita and I walk a little ways away to say our goodbyes. It is all so frantic that she does not have time to get misty-eyed, and I put down the lump in my chest. A last kiss and a promise to write even more often and she is waving from the backseat as the car pulls away. The mother's car pulls out with them and I am suddenly alone.

I am overwhelmed with loneliness and melancholy. I don't want to stay downtown as I had planned. I walk back along Fourth Street. Leaves have started to fall and collect in the gutters. Now the city seems to be dying. I sing the sad words of "September Song" and hear the crunch of leaves under my feet. I am at a loss as to what to do with myself.

Chapter 16

Down at the far end of Bertha's corridor in the small front wing of the main building three salesmen have their offices. Just before you come to them you encounter their secretaries who share a large office of their own. Nadine, Doris, and Irma are their names and they look like a Nadine, Doris, and Irma. Nadine and Doris are in their late thirties and stout. I think that they are both married. They don't seem much motivated by their jobs. Irma is slightly younger and shy. The two older women have apparently taken her under their wings. They are always giving her advice about men, where to live, what to wear, and how to deal with her boss.

On my last mail run of the morning I stop by to see if they have any outgoing mail. There seems to be little correspondence to or from them. But they have an aura of busyness about them. I wonder if they are typing personal letters. Their bosses are seldom in the plant.

Doris asks me if I have been to the movies, and I tell her I have seen *Lili* with Leslie Caron. It is a charming bit of fluff with a song that has gotten popular and it has served as a starring vehicle for the gaminesque Miss Caron and for Zsa Zsa Gabor just after her success in *Moulin Rouge*. Jean Pierre Aumont is a sleazy magician and Mel Ferrar is a puppeteer.

"Oh, I saw that," Doris gushes. "Wasn't it wonderful?"

"I liked it," I say.

Nadine looks up. "What's that?"

"We are talking about the movie, *Lili*. Have you seen it?"

"No, what is it about?"

Doris quickly outlines the circus premise and plunges into the plot. "So Mel Ferrar plays this crippled puppeteer who loves her. But the little cluck can't see him for this slimy magician who is already married anyway."

"I like magic acts and magicians," Irma contributes.

"You have to see it. Anyway, Lili wakes up at last and falls in love with the puppeteer who gets over his lameness."

I wonder how closely she was watching the movie. In a dream sequence he is no longer lame. But it is a moment of clarity when Lili can see past his deformity to the man beneath. I don't try to correct Doris. Every person should take what he or she can from a movie.

In my first mail run after lunch I find Nadine preparing to leave for the day to attend a funeral. She is in a quandary because she has not been able to reach her boss to let him know she is going.

"He thinks that I am back here taking care of things," she agitates. "What if something comes up and he needs to reach somebody here?"

"Then I'll connect him," Doris says. "Really, Nadine, there is nothing that he would want you to do that I haven't done a hundred times myself or Irma too, for that matter."

"Oh, no. Don't let Irma talk to him." Irma blanches and Nadine is quick to apologize. "I know you could handle it, Hon, but my boss can be a bear sometimes."

"You go on. You'll be late. It'll be okay," Doris reassures her.

I wonder about the lateness of the hour. Funerals are usually held in the morning or no later than about noon. And then everybody comes back to the house and eats and consoles the family. It will be hot out at the cemetery. Maybe they do things differently down here in Louisville. When I leave the office, Irma is complaining about Nadine's lack of confidence in her.

When I enter the office a couple hours later, the telephone on Nadine's desk is ringing and Irma is on her feet and looks about to flee. Doris is nowhere to be seen.

"Woodie! It's Nadine's phone."

"Yes. Aren't you going to answer it?"

"I can't. It's probably Mr. Morris. Doris went to the bathroom. Do you see her out there?"

I can see all the way down the corridor back to Mr. Gerlach's office. No help is coming for Irma.

"She's not in sight. You will have to take it, Irma," I advise.

She walks to Nadine's desk and looks at the telephone as if it is a snake. She hesitates and then reaches to pick it up. She cringes with dread. She forgets to say, "Mr. Morris's office," and instead merely says, "Hello."

I can hear Mr. Morris's angry voice coming through the earpiece. He has been kept waiting for nine or ten rings. Then his secretary has not picked up, and he has gotten this young incompetent who he believes is incapable of assisting him.

"She isn't here," I hear her say.

I hear him shout for an explanation.

"She had to attend a funeral," she stammers. "I think it was an aunt on her mother's side."

Mr. Morris does not want this kind of information. He asks for Doris. Irma tells him that she has gone to the restroom. He tells her to put the telephone down and go find her. She does so and flees down the corridor. There is no mail to pick up. I gaze dumbly at the telephone. I wonder where Mr. Morris is calling from and what emergency he could have that he needs to talk to Nadine or Doris.

Doris comes flying into the room and picks up the telephone. After the initial greeting she doesn't talk. She is making notes on a tablet. Irma slides into the room and presses herself against the wall beside the door. She looks about to flee again. Tears have welled up in her eyes. I wonder that she has messed up. Surely she could have taken a message from Mr. Morris. She probably just panicked. I know the feeling. I'm sure that Doris will calm her down and handle whatever has come up. And Mr. Morris will be sorry for the way he blew up at her. I take my mailbag and slip on up the corridor myself. I have the mail to get out.

Mr. Poulter gets the chance to sell the farm at Miller Station for a profit. He buys another between Paris and Georgetown in Bourbon County and wants my father as the tenant. They work out the details, and we are on the move once again. It is a grand house and on a large acreage of gentle fields and rolling slopes unlike the farms have been in Nicholas County.

We attend Center Hill High School. All of the county students in Nicholas County had attended Headquarters. Here in Bourbon there are four county schools, and we get all the students in the western side of the county. It is not so traumatic for us this time to change. The school seems smaller somehow, but each class is housed in a separate room so the teachers don't have to switch back and forth between two classes.

My teacher is Miss Crouch. What a grouch! She doesn't know of my past medical history and doesn't favor me at all. We don't get on very well. When I don't know the capital of Mongolia, I have to stay in at recess and write "The capital of Mongolia is Urga" 1,000 times.

We have a short school bus ride. Odell and Clyde are both with us, so Jimmy and I have less work to do around the farm. But we still have to help with the tobacco bed weeding, the planting, the hoeing, the housing, and the stripping. After Odell leaves, we want Clyde to take us to a basketball game. The only way he will do it is if we promise to get up early every morning and help him with the milking and hog feeding and other chores. So after that we have to get up when he does.

The house is a fine old ante-bellum structure. It has ornate woodwork inside with a big circular staircase leading up from the front hall. To the left downstairs and upstairs is a single large room. We use the downstairs room as our living room. To the right is another large room which we make into a dining room and never go into. Each room has a large chandelier and somewhere in the past these two rooms were used to host large dinner parties.

The Poulters ask to put some things in the nice room upstairs. Mom and Pop think they are going to place some of their extra furniture in it and agree. But the Poulters merely want to use it for storage. They bring boxes of junk to get it out of their house. We see them take it in. And then they lock it to keep us kids out. Pop is indignant that they have taken one of our best rooms for this purpose. We mostly live in the rooms of an "L" that has been added running back off the right side. The kitchen and sitting room are in it. Upstairs of it are two bedrooms and we can go up from the kitchen climbing a boxed-in stairway.

There is a long side porch that also has an upstairs. It is my hiding place. I have discovered reading. But we are in the crops nearly every day. My greatest pleasure on a rainy day is to hide out with a book on the upstairs part of the porch to read and listen to the music from the radio downstairs.

I have a little money and decide to buy some records. Juanita has left me her little phonograph. But I only have a few records that she owns and have nearly worn them out playing them over and over. The only one of my own is "Perfidia" by Ben Light, the piano player. The first time I heard it Clyde and I were driving through Paris on the way to get some tobacco plants. Later I heard it in Newberry's and bought it. Good records cost 99 cents. But there are several companies that put out cheap imitations to cover popular songs. They hire sound-alike groups and their records sell for as little as 59 cents.

We are at the end of the Big Band era, but I don't know that. I like Tommy Dorsey and Glen Miller and singers like Vaughn Monroe and Frankie Laine. I have always liked off-the-wall stuff like Spike Jones. We had a record of his during the war called "Right in the Fuhrer's Face" that we wore out playing over and over. Now I am into more romantic ballads. On the farm we listened to the Hit Parade every week with Snookie Lanson.

When I started going with Juanita "Blue Tango" was popular, and so was "Delicado" and "Poinciana" and "Plink, Plank, Plunk." The latter song is by Bobby Maxwell playing a harp. He makes the harp sound like a piano. I like Les Paul and Mary Ford and their multiple recordings. They have several songs out this summer. And Rosemary Clooney and Guy Mitchell are racking up a lot of hits.

Downtown Louisville has several record stores. They leave their doors open and let the music drift out into the street. Maybe someone will walk by and be drawn into the store to buy a recording that they hear. The stores have air conditioning units in the back. They run them with big fans that circulate the cool air and let it flow on out the front door. The cool air is delicious and inviting to anyone passing on the street. I enter to browse around before the movie I have come downtown to see starts.

Frank Sinatra has a record out "The Moon was Yellow" that I really like, but I cannot find it. Similarly, I cannot find Carmen McRae's "Star Eyes." But I get Glen Miller's recordings of "Perfidia" and "At Last" and Jimmy Dorsey's recordings of "Green Eyes" and "The Breeze and I." On the JD records, Bob Eberle and Helen O'Connell share the vocals.

I walk around with my purchases. They are playing the latest hits. Patti Page's "Tennessee Waltz" drives me crazy. I never liked it to start with. It has been a big popular country hit. And then it rose to the top of the popular charts. So I have endured it twice. It seems that it will never go away. I hear June Valli's "Crying in the Chapel" and a song called "No Other Love Have I." It is a hit for Perry Como. It has been written by Richard Rodgers and used as theme music in the television series *Victory at Sea*. Later it is featured in the movie *Second Chance* which I see in 3-D. It is a nice song, but I can only afford a few records and that is not among my selections.

I don't have a lot of time to listen to music on the radio as I often did during my idle hours on the farm. When I enter restaurants, I usually look over the jukebox selections to see what they have. I seldom put money into them. But I sometimes play Johnnie and Jack's "Down in the Caribbean" and "Big Mamoo" in Tony's Restaurant. If you frequent a restaurant a lot and listen to the jukebox that others are feeding, you feel obligated to plug some dimes into it once in a while yourself.

At night I listen to the records over and over again with the volume turned low. Someday I am going to own a fine collection of music. I keep my new records in their dust jackets and keep them in a drawer so they won't be affected by the heat. I am always on the lookout to increase my collection.

When I am four or five, I lose my baby teeth. One of my front teeth does not come out. The new, bigger tooth pushes out in front of it and for a few days the old one is loose and should have been pulled out. I worry it with my tongue and fingers, and Clyde offers to jerk it. But I think he may be rough and I am afraid. The tooth tightens back up and I am left with a double tooth.

Of course, I can't get between them with a toothbrush and over the new few years decay sets in between the teeth. We only brush sporadically anyway. There is no running water in the house so you have to take your brush and toothpaste, or powder, and a dipper of water and go out back to do the brushing. There are no protective chemicals in the water like fluoride. Everybody in the family has bad teeth. Mom and Pop have dentures. It is accepted that everyone loses their teeth by the time they are thirty.

Jimmy and I are rough-housing in the yard and I smash my mouth against something. The double tooth, the old one, in back is cracked. I am in pain. It is time for my first trip to the dentist. Pop takes me to Dr. Bates who has his practice on the second floor of the Agriculture Bank Building in Paris where he does his banking. It is a three-story building and is the first time I have ridden in an elevator. A black man in uniform takes us up. He is very formal and solicitous that we don't get caught in the doors. Few people go up to the offices on the floors above the bank. The elevator operator is idle much of the day.

Dr. Bates is an old dentist and has been practicing in the town for many years. That is how Pop has come to know him. He is not up on the latest techniques. His drill is slow and excruciating. He has a hypodermic needle for applying Novocain that must date from the previous century. It has a long coarse needle and hurts like the devil. When he pulls the baby tooth out, he finds decay in the back of my permanent tooth and says that he will have to drill it out and fill it.

I think he will use Novocain to deaden the tooth, but I am mistaken. He says it will injure the tooth. He goes in and drills the tooth without deadening it. The rot is deep. He has to drill through the nerve. When he hits the nerve I am propelled out of my seat. I try to push his arm and the drill away. I cannot stand it. He admonishes me for my interference. He gives me a minute to recover my composure.

My father is embarrassed by my actions. He and the dentist discuss it like I am not even there.

"I know it gives him discomfort," says Dr. Bates, "but it has to be done."

"He's not very strong," says my father. "He's always been a little chicken-hearted."

I cannot believe that such libel has come out of my father's mouth. How can he watch it and not realize the pain I am going through? Has he so little regard for me?

The dentist tells him that he should come in and get some work done on his own teeth.

"Maybe later in the fall," he replies. "After the hot weather is over."

The call from the FBI does not come. I am starting to think that I will be here in Louisville over the winter. It will be cold delivering the mail. I have a heavy jacket back at the farm. I will have to bring it to Louisville. But just now we are slowly moving into fall and except for the mornings being crisp, the days are much like summer. Back on the farm we would be wrapping up our tobacco housing and getting ready to strip the leaves. I wonder who Clyde will get to help him.

A better solution for me would be to move into another job at the plant. I haven't actively pursued this because I was counting on the job at the FBI to come through. I begin to make discreet enquiries into openings around the plant. Jones-Dabney is a good place to work. I haven't known anyone to leave since I came to work in the spring. I don't even know where I would want to work in the plant. Maybe Forrest will get something else, and I can move into his position in Personnel.

My days fall into a symphony of sameness. I write to Juanita several times each week. I receive letters from her regularly. She is still sharing an apartment with two other girls. They have a kitchen and can cook and entertain. She says one of the other girls has boyfriends, but she is waiting for me. I pick up my mail and go out to eat. Most nights I return to listen to the radio until bedtime. The Colonels have made the playoffs. I think about trying to go out to a game.

Football season starts. I try to pick up the Kentucky games but am unable to do so. The University of Louisville plays at a lower level than does Kentucky, but they have an excellent quarterback named Johnny Unitas who will take them to a winning season. I listen to some of the games but don't seem to be able to get caught up in it.

I prowl the streets on weekends and before dark in the evenings. I am melancholy. I sing "I'll Go My Way by Myself" from *Bandwagon*. I have no social friends. I walk and daydream. I hold conversations in my head. I replay movies I have seen. I see each several times and can remember the dialogue very well. I put myself into them. I still want to be a writer. I am plodding through *For Whom the Bell Tolls.* I think I could write like Hemingway, but where do I get the kinds of experiences that would be interesting to people to read about?

A letter comes from Juanita. She says that she has heard from Wilma Jo. She and Carl have returned to Nicholas County and have reconciled with her parents. They have taken an apartment in Carlisle on Main Street over one of the stores. I know the sort of place they have. Seedy and rundown. Probably worse than where they lived here in Louisville. Carl is taking on odd work. Wilma Jo has told Juanita that he is painting houses. I hope they are going to make it.

Finally, the day arrives when a letter is awaiting me on the table just inside the foyer. It has the seal of the FBI on it. I try to close my mind until I can open it. I suppose it could be thanks but no thanks, we are not hiring just now. But that doesn't prove to be the case. This is just what I have been waiting for. They have taken their time, but it is a request for me to come into their local office to interview for a job.

In the summer of 1947 everyone is talking about flying saucers. They are being seen everywhere, but mostly out west. The paper recounts stories of sightings. An air force plane has chased one, but it kept going up and he couldn't reach it because of the altitude. Military people and civil aviation experts explain away some of the incidents, but they keep pouring in. It has only been a few years since Orson Welles's

"War of the Worlds" broadcast, and the invention of the atomic bomb and tales of the effects of radiation on rats and other animals make everybody ready to believe we may be ready to be attacked by people from another planet.

Clyde is a big reader of science-fiction stories. I have read a lot of them too in his pulp magazines. He speculates on what it all means. It is maddening to him that they can't catch one of these things or shoot it down. People have had encounters with the little beings that ride in the machines. But most are kooks, or religious nuts who are proclaiming the end of the world. They vastly outnumber the ones who aren't.

After supper, we lie out on the bank beside the well and watch the sky. We are well away from the glow of any city lights. The stars light up the sky. They are up there by the tens of thousands. The Milky Way is like a great wide highway stretching across the great expanse above us. We don't know the stars, but can pick out the North Star and the Big and Little Dippers. One or the other of us occasionally spots a moving light that proves to be an early evening aircraft wending its way east or west. Airline traffic is starting to increase in these days after the war although the railroads still account for most of the passenger miles.

But people are mostly curious. They aren't panicked by the reports. We have just been through a war with Hitler and the Japanese. What could be scarier than that? Maybe we just don't know what to do with peace. Everybody is back from overseas except for our occupation forces. Everybody is employed building houses and automobiles and more factories. The returning military have married and are starting families. Experts glumly warn that the world cannot support such a population boom. But other reports recount the great losses of lives in Russia and Germany where many women will not be able to find husbands.

Germany and Japan have been devastated. Millions of Jews have been killed. Russia has proved to be as evil as Germany. They have grabbed off all the countries in Eastern Europe and imposed their system. We have finally had to confront them over Austria and Berlin. This time we aren't going to be caught sleeping like we were at Pearl Harbor. Some politicians want to reinstate the draft. It is predicted that we will soon be at war with Russia or China or maybe both.

So we wait and watch the stars. Maybe we long for a people with more intelligence than we have to come down to Earth and clean up our mess.

* * *

Juanita and Lynwood (1953)

* * *

Chapter 17

In 1953 the FBI still enjoys the prestige it has garnered through the years of fighting big crime and staving off Japanese and Nazi saboteurs in World War II. They have been glamorized in films like *G-Men*, *Dillinger*, and *The House on 92nd Street*. J. Edgar Hoover is ever conscious of the Bureau's image and he effectively squelches criticism and sees that its every success is publicized. The legends have sprung up through the stories of Dillinger and "the lady in red," Pretty Boy Floyd, Machine Gun Kelly, and Al Capone. Their investigations into the Lindberg Kidnapping and participation in the Kansas City Massacre are still fresh in the public's minds. Its capture of Japanese espionage messages and apprehension of German saboteurs intent on crippling American industry has been followed by similar exploits in the cold war. The cases of Hiss and Klaus Fuchs and the theft of the atomic secrets have been prominently reported and the Rosenberg and Greenglass cases are further evidence that the FBI is a vital guardian against communism.

The men out front are Hoover and his agents. But backing them up is a vast bureaucracy of fingerprint experts, chemical analysts, cryptanalysts, and handwriting experts. The successes of the Bureau give Hoover almost a free hand to build his establishment as his vision drives it. The Washington Headquarters is said to have over 8,000 employees with 4,000 more out in Field and Regional Offices all over the country.

The Louisville Field Office services most of Kentucky and southern Indiana. The agents assigned here are mostly looking for draft dodgers and deserters from the services. There is little big crime for them to fight, and corporate crime that infringes on federal statutes is more often a matter for the Treasury Department. They have offices in a large building on Third Street. A clothing store is on the first floor. I walk through to the elevators in the back and read the sign that identifies the occupants of each floor.

I am stalling. As I approach the interview, my heart and bowels are clutched by the cold hand of fear and dread. All my future is riding on the next few minutes, I think. The agent interviewer may size me up as completely unsuitable and send me away with vague promises to be in touch. Send me away back to a life of delivering envelopes to the employees of Jones-Dabney. I have no other prospects. I have everything riding on this interview and getting this job.

I have to show confidence. I have to appear interested in the FBI and focused on the job. I have rehearsed what I think I will be asked. "Why do you want to work for the FBI?" I will state my high regard for the Bureau and my impressions when I visited their headquarters in Washington on my Senior trip. "What would you like to do at the Bureau?" I want to get a good clerical position while I enter college part-time and work to get a degree so I can satisfy the requirements to become an agent. "Is there anything in your background that could prevent the Bureau from hiring you?" They mean arrests or drug use. I can truthfully answer negatively. Besides, I know that they have already interviewed teachers and neighbors. I take a deep breath and push the button to call the elevator.

The FBI offices occupy the entire fourth floor of the building. Along one side are two glass-enclosed cubicles. The agents who I take to be in charge of the office can sit in these and see everyone in the office. Agents and clerks and typists seem to be randomly seated about the large room. Pillars support the ceiling. Otherwise, no other partitions exist. As I come into the room, I am greeted by a young man who occupies a desk adjacent to the door. I show him my letter. He directs me to an agent sitting not far away. He is in a shirt and tie. The pants he is wearing are undoubtedly part of a good suit. He has stripped the coat off on the warm day. I am similarly attired in my only white shirt and tie. I have worn a sports coat. My only suit is a double-breasted affair that I think is out of date.

He tells me his name is Kelly and he will talk to me, although my letter has been sent out by the Agent in Charge. Kelly is obviously busy and has other things on his mind. But he goes through the motions of the interview and he asks the questions that I anticipate. My only question in turn is whether I will work in Washington or here in Louisville. He says that there are currently no openings here in Louisville, but they are in need of clerical help in Washington. He says that after I am hired on I may be able to arrange a transfer back to Louisville if that is my wish. I am perfectly satisfied to be going to Washington.

He tells me very little about the job. I may be involved in fingerprint identification or some laboratory or communications group depending on the need. He tells me of the entry salary and other benefits such as leave and health care. He gives me another questionnaire to fill out and a medical form for a physical. I need to bring both of these back or I can just mail them in. If there are no glitches, they should be contacting me about reporting in just a few weeks. We shake hands and I leave walking on air. I fairly run back up the street to the bus stop. I need to get back to work to get out the end of the day mail. All the way back on the bus I read the questionnaire and medical form over and over. I am that close to leaving for a career with the FBI in Washington.

Norman Wright and I are messing around in the schoolyard after lunch. It is almost time for the bell to ring for us to return to our rooms. *Eddie Fitzgerald runs by. He tells us to come on. They are having a snowball fight with some high school guys.*

There is a little courtyard between the gym where the lunchroom is located and the main building. Some seventh graders and a couple high school guys have traded snowballs on the way back from lunch. More seventh graders have swarmed to help our classmates and soon we have the high school boys outgunned. They hold on grimly and Mr. Sheldon, the principal, watches from a window in the hall. Some other high school boys walk by him and he chides them for allowing their classmates to be abused by these seventh graders. The seventh grade seems to give him more trouble than all the other classes put together. He is not fond of us.

Some more high school kids rally to their aid and soon word spreads around the school about the big snowball fight. All the high school boys join in. I see my brother, Jimmy, among them. Now we are the ones outnumbered. But we are stubborn and fight on. The big boys like John Lee Hash and Ed Fitzgerald and Norman Yazell move up close and take snowballs in the face to get good accuracy on their own throws.

I do not have a good throwing arm and the snow is well chewed up where they are confronting each other. So I retire a little ways and make myself busy molding snowballs for the others. They rush back to me, gather four or five of my snowballs and run back into the fight. Mr. Sheldon is our only spectator. He gleefully watches the seventh graders getting pounded. He lets it run on and does not sound the bell ending lunchtime.

My pal, Norman, has an idea. The high schoolers are positioned beside the walkway that runs from the gym to the main building. It is an open walkway and if some of us go around the school, we can catch the high school guys in a crossfire. Four of us gather up a load of snowballs and run around the schoolhouse. We are almost there when we meet some high schoolers coming toward us. They have had the same idea.

We have a fierce brief fight. We expend all our snowballs and give up. They tell us that we can't go back to the fight. We have to go into the building. Else they will hold us down and rub our faces in the snow. We have to agree to their demands.

Just then the bell rings calling us back in. We tell Miss Davis and the girls about our big snowball fight. It is hard to make it sound heroic. It has started by us picking on a few high schoolers. And I find out that after we four left the others broke and fled when the rest of the high schoolers charged them. Mr. Sheldon rang the bell after the fight moved away. It is most disappointing to us to know that we aren't liked in the school, but we have a lot of good esprit de corps in our class.

When Wilma Jo and Carl came to Louisville to get married, they had to get a blood test and examination before they could get their marriage license. They had gone to a doctor near the City Clerk's office. They told us in hilarious terms of the amusing Dr. Fawcett, who had to be 70 years old and without much of a practice. He is the doctor I want to see.

My bout with rheumatic fever when I was a youngster has left me with a heart murmur. My family doctor, Dr. Hart, has closely monitored it throughout my lifetime and has always cautioned me for the need to avoid stress and overexertion. Dr. Hart is the only physician I have been to since I can remember, but I don't want him filling out the papers for the FBI. They might turn me down because of my heart murmur. The deaf and nearly senile Dr. Fawcett suits my purposes fine.

I don't know how bad my heart murmur is. Maybe it will be evident to even Dr. Fawcett, but Dr. Hart in my most recent visit has told me that it is improving.

I find his office in a decrepit building in downtown Louisville. I think the rent here cannot be very dear. I have to walk up two flights. He has a small anteroom but no receptionist or nurse.

He is a one-man business. I figure he is just doing this to stay occupied. Probably he has lost his wife and is at loose ends. This way at least some of his old patients drop by from time-to-time to talk and stay in touch.

He comes out of the inner office to see who has come in. He is surprised to see me. Probably he was getting ready to go home or go out to dinner. I tell him of my need for an examination and for him to fill in the blanks on the FBI medical report. He is delighted to have me and ushers me into his office. His equipment and examination table don't look that out of date. Maybe I have misjudged. But in my long experience with doctors I have almost always been kept waiting.

He wants to know how I have come to choose him. I tell him I am new to the town and my friends Wilma Jo and Carl have recommended him. He is pleased that he is getting word-of-mouth publicity, but he doesn't remember them. He takes my blood pressure and listens to my heart first thing. My blood pressure is on the low side as it usually is. I try to stay calm and keep my heart steady. He does not comment on it. He listens to my lungs. They have cleared now from the bronchitis that I have had earlier in the year. He asks me if I have had any serious medical problems in the past that he should note. I tell him I cannot think of any.

I try to keep him talking to keep him distracted. He is pleased to have someone to talk to who is interested in his practice. He plods through the list of questions. He notes my heart rate and does not write any other comment. I think I am home free. He gives me a little bottle and tells me to give him a urine sample. There is no bathroom in the office. I wonder where he goes during the day. I will have to do it in front of him. I am pee-shy. I always have trouble urinating in front of others. He realizes it immediately and walks away and pretends to be busy at something on his table. I finally manage a small amount. He says it will be enough. He will have to send it out to get it analyzed. I can come back tomorrow when he will have the results and get the completed form.

I can pay him then, he says. It will be twelve dollars. I have been here less than an hour. Pretty good pay, I think. But worth it to me. I have pulled a fast one. The FBI won't know anything about my heart. They think they will be getting a prime specimen. And that's what I am, really.

Miss Davis wants the seventh grade class to put on a Christmas play for the school. We are a big class of around 35, but there are enough parts for everyone what with Herod's court, and soldiers, the holy family, wise men, shepherds, angels, and chorus. She has found the play in a magazine, and she has everyone copy down their lines. My pal, Norman Wright, gets a swell part as the Lord High Chancellor. I am to be one of the soldiers. I am devastated. I want a speaking part.

I should be one of the wise men since I have such a good singing voice, but no one here at Center Hill knows it. I am a bit short and that is why she has not considered me for one of the important roles. She has visualized all this somehow, for most of the roles are for boys, and she has cast some real dunderheads in them.

Jackie Sargent is as miffed as I am. He is to be the second shepherd. He has three or four lines. He does not want to do it. He prefers the anonymity of standing around as a soldier guard. I see my chance. I take him to see Miss Davis and ask if we can swap roles. She is being harried by everyone seeking changes or explaining why they might not be in town to do it. She agrees to our change without a word and I gleefully get a paper to copy down my part.

Charles Redmond and Ray Lizer are the other two shepherds. We have one whole scene to ourselves where we see the star and meet the angels and another scene with most of the cast at the stable. Miss Davis tells us to bring in our bathrobes for our costumes on the day of the play. I sleep in my underwear and don't own a bathrobe. It is a non-crisis. Norman will lend me one of his. It is a little big on me, but Miss Davis is pleased. It looks more like a loose garment that would be worn every day. One of the girls fashions me a turban out of a piece of cloth that looks like a baby blanket. How does she know how to do that?

John Lee Hash has talked himself out of the play and Miss Davis makes him stage manager. For our scene he builds a little pile of kindling in the center of the stage with a red light bulb to simulate a fire. In all the scenes a large electric star from somebody's Christmas decorations hangs in the right background of the stage.

It all goes grand. Charles stumbles over one line, but it is scarcely noticed. After I do my lines: "Yonder lies Bethlehem. See the dim lights of the dwellings? Soon the people will sleep in their beds under their roofs, while we shall lie out here under the brightly shining stars till we sleep," we pause while the chorus sings "Little Town of Bethlehem."

I have another line with God in it, which embarrasses me to say. Miss Davis has earlier told me to say it with more enthusiasm. So I belt out "Glory be to God! We shall see the new king!" I am pleased with my performance. The school likes it too. And Miss Davis is happy it has gone off well.

When we come off the stage, the students are all filing out of the gym going back to their rooms where they will share presents and get some candy before being released early to catch the buses home for Christmas vacation. My brother, Jimmy, and Tommy Rankin, both ninth graders, are standing by the steps smiling and nodding at people praising the play. They have been mistaken for members of our class. They think it is a great lark, but my classmates are indignant that they are stealing our praise.

I am optimistic now about getting out of Kentucky and going to Washington, D.C. It is a place I have heard about all my life.

That I have seen in movies and heard about on the radio. It is where the news comes from every night. It is where the big events of the world are happening. People say it is the most important city in the world eclipsing London and Paris and New York. World figures stroll its streets. I may be passing J. Edgar Hoover in the halls everyday just as I see Mr. Gerlach now.

I am dying to let someone know that I am this close to a new career in a big, exciting town. About to take on an important role with an important organization. But what if I crow about it and something happens so that it doesn't come true? First, I will look silly. Second, it will poison my relations with the Jones-Dabney people since they will know that I am trying to leave. It is better to stay silent about it for now. When and if they call me I will have time to give Mr. Gerlach my two-week notice and give him time to find a replacement. It is always better to leave on good terms with everyone.

Before I received my letter for the interview, we had been talking about the company basketball team. They play in an industrial league here in Louisville. I take it that they want plenty of players in case some don't show up for particular games. I always wanted to play with an organized team. I only went out for basketball one year in high school and that was after my father died. It was too late to make the team. But I still yearn to play. Now I know that I will be going to Washington, and I will not get to play with the team from Jones-Dabney, but when the first practice comes up, Jimmy Andrews asks me if I don't want to come out and try out for the team.

I have Clyde's old green bathing suit to run around in. I pack it in my little gym bag that I carry in to the farm every other weekend and wait for Jimmy to pick me up near the park. He has Earl Logan with him. Earl is one of the laborers pushing the drums of paint around in shipping. It appears that everyone is going to get a fair shot at making the team.

John Bigelow from over in the R & D Building is coaching. I gather that he has served in the same role last season and has allowed himself to be talked into it again. Nearly all the young men in Kentucky are well versed in basketball and we could probably play without a coach, or any one of us could take over the duties. But it is a thankless job, and we are glad to have John to do it.

We are a pretty non-descript team. We are without a good center. I think of all the big guys among the Negro workers in the paint shed. We could sure use some of them. But this is a segregated league. I wonder if the Negroes have a league of their own. Jones-Dabney could probably field a pretty good team with its black paint shed workers.

We don't have all our players out. We divide into two four-man teams and scrimmage. John says to use it for conditioning. In the next practice he will start working on some plays and making sure we know our defenses. In Kentucky we hate zone defenses. In man-to-man you can tell who is guarding their man and who isn't. I am small and light on my feet. I can always stay with my man.

Jimmy Andrews is surprisingly good. He plays guard and is self-assured of his ability. He reminds my of my classmate, Donnie Gaunce, who has led the Nicholas County team all through high school and is now on scholarship at Morehead State University. Earl Logan is pretty good too. But we have to have better players than this or we or not going to fare well in the league. A pickup team among my classmates at school could have beaten Jones-Dabney.

As he drives me back to my room, Jimmy discusses the scrimmage and our chances in the coming season. It is obvious that Jones-Dabney is not going to be embarrassed. Apparently, it is customary for John to bring out a few mercenaries to strengthen the team. Jimmy thinks four or five such talents are needed. I feel better about it all. My leaving is not going to squelch my chances of playing a lot of basketball for this team. I would have been on the bench behind a bunch of ringers.

Jimmy drops me off and we say we'll see each other in the morning. I know my muscles will be sore during my mail runs. I want to wish them good luck on the upcoming season. I suppose there will be no way to stay in touch and find out how they fare. If I get to Washington by November, perhaps they have teams at the FBI I can play for.

Chapter 18

St. James and Belgravia Courts sit on the site of the former Southern Exposition of 1883-1887. The exposition was essentially the World Fair of the time. President Chester A. Arthur himself opened it in 1883 and it ran annually for five years. It highlighted the innovations of the day and touted the rebirth of southern industry. Thomas Edison threw the switch to activate the lighting which was the largest display to be found anywhere outside New York City. Electric trolley cars were also seen for the first time and took the delighted passengers through lighted tunnels around the grounds of the exposition and the nearby Dupont estate.

At the end of the exposition, the buildings were dismantled and in their places St. James and Belgravia Courts were born. They are at once the most beautiful and recognizable areas of the city. On St. James Court, stately Victorian homes make an oval frame around two lush shaded greens centered by a magnificent bronze statue. Belgravia and Fountain Courts are "walking courts" with homes facing each other across a park-like green, away from traffic and other urban noise. At night the area is lit by the soft glow of gaslight. It is a setting to sooth the soul.

During my stay in Louisville and my weeks working at Jones-Dabney, I have always cut through St. James Court on my way to the Post Office at Fifth and Lee each morning. The growth of old oaks line the sidewalks and you move as though beneath a canopy or tunnel. Now into October its loveliness is further enhanced by the rustic turn of leaves and their gentle carpeting of the walkways. I go along kicking the leaves and whistling or humming.

The sun seems to fade as we move into fall. There is a sharpness in the air at night. The days are shorter. In the evenings it is dark before I get home from the plant. But on the weekends I walk with my feelings and emotions. I dream of melancholy things – of girls and sorrow and tragedy. The dying leaves turn and give up their lives in a final splash of yellow or orange. The wind twitches the leaves and moves them toward the gutter. The air smells sweet of the dying foliage and a faint smell of burning somewhere far off.

I hum the popular songs of the time like "September Song" and "Autumn Leaves." I sing Johnny Mercer's "Early Autumn" about someone who holds memories of his summer love and looks through frosted windowpanes at falling leaves and a town grown cold such as my town has become.

The dying leaves seem to inspire in me a sadness. Everything seems to be ending. The summer that had started out so perfectly is ending. It is the autumn of my perfect year. The days are growing short and each day is a day that will never be again on Earth. Maybe I could write about it someday. And capture my feeling as the poets did.

The frost in the air seems to add a shine to everything. And the smell seems to be made up of parts of the river and the mountains to the east. It is as if their fragrances are borne upon the breezes. I breathe in great draughts of the air. I will remember the sounds of the city after I leave, and I will remember the smells.

The sun is traversing lower above the trees in Central Park. The shadows creep far out beyond where I had sat to watch the tennis matches. There is a sameness about the oaks around the park, but the decorative trees in people's yards light up with reds and oranges of sourgum, scarlet of maple, and yellow ash. I think of the riot of colors we would have now back on the farm. Of the sunlight on autumn fields. Of the tobacco recently housed turning golden in the barns. Of goldenrod and thistle and milkweed swelling and bursting forth their seed. To be carried away by the wind. To spread and root and bring forth new life in the spring. I think of the walnuts and hickory nuts to be gathered. And the Indian Cigars lying about beneath the Catalpa trees to be secretly smoked. I lie back and look at the long, low, lazy skies. I am lulled by the drowsy hum of insects living the ends of their lives.

I can't imagine what my childhood would have been had I not had Jimmy as an older brother. He is almost three years older than me and, though I am small for my age, he is almost a midget. Mom frets over him, but nothing she does results in any kind of a growth spurt. He is only two years ahead of me in school, however. But I nearly overtake him in height. Mom dresses us like twins for a while. But we really don't have a facial resemblance. You can see some of Mom and some of Pop in my face. Jimmy is dark and doesn't look very much like others in the family except maybe Geneva. He is furious if you remark that he looks like her. He doesn't like her since she is always trying to correct him.

It is great to have a brother two years ahead of me in school. He can always tell me what to expect in the grades coming up. I am a better scholar than Jimmy, but he doesn't have anyone paving the way for him. The moments when I can find him on the playground are treasured by me. But he is always there for me when I get home. We go out to play, and he tells me exaggerated stories of what has transpired in his school day.

The big farms are our playgrounds. We run here and there investigating everything. Odell and Clyde are gone to the army. Robert and Lloyd should have been with us during the war and looked out for us, but they are in Highland Cemetery. Mom and Pop are busy with the farm and haven't got much time to spend with us. We pretty much raise ourselves. We gain a world of self-reliance except that it is so insular on the farm that it is hard for us to meet and mix with strangers.

After I have my bout with rheumatic fever, I am pretty much put under a deathwatch and most of the tasks and chores around the farm fall on Jimmy. He is shouldering a man's workload before he gets to high school. Pop comes down hard on him. He gives him some bad beatings for one offense or another. I wish I could be more protective of him, but I am afraid of Pop myself when these furies come over him. At school Jimmy looks out for me and fights a couple bullies who are picking on me.

We are inseparable in our young lives. Two events, happening almost simultaneously, cause us to drift apart later. The first is that Jimmy graduates two years ahead of me. Now we don't ride the school bus together and don't have as much time to spend together. Then Pop dies the summer he gets out of school. He spends more time with Clyde running the farm. They do things and plan their days not taking me into account. I still share a bed with Jimmy, but he is becoming a stranger to me.

The Korean War is on and Jimmy is about to be drafted. He enlists so that he will get to pick his field. After boot camp he is shipped to Hawaii and then to Germany instead of Korea. He is finally having some luck. He comes home on leave. He has sprouted up some since leaving high school. He is now near normal height. He has filled out on army food and cuts quite a handsome figure in his uniform. But he is someone I no longer know.

As I am cutting across St. James on an aimless mission, I am hailed from one of the Victorian houses. A man and woman stand before the house with a sofa. They seem to be jockeying it toward the door. The man tells me that he has bought the sofa from a neighbor and needs to get it into the house. It only needs to go up three or four steps and into the living room which is the first room through the door. They have moved it from the house next door, but the woman does not have the strength to carry an end of it up the stairs. They wonder if I will help.

The woman looks at me dubiously now that she sees me closer. She probably outweighs me by fifty pounds. But I still retain my farm strength. I tell them I will be happy to help. Just up the stairs, he says.

The sofa is not overly heavy. It is not like picking up the corner of a farm wagon to fix a wheel, or wrestling around a turning plow or cutting harrow. I take the leading end and back up the steps letting the man carry his end forward. The woman hurries to hold the door. We get the sofa to the landing and the man tells me to rest. We set it down. I am not the least bit tired, but after all, he has brought it all the way from next door.

"Will it fit through the door?" I ask.

"We measured it. It will just fit through," he assures me.

I am doubtful. We try it and sure enough, it will not go through. We will have to tilt it. This makes it harder to handle. We will have to twist it through. I haven't looked to see which way the door swings.

"Stop," I say. "We will have to take it back out and tilt it the other way to twist it around the door facing."

"No, this is working okay," he insists. He is red in the face and doesn't want to stop now.

"We won't be able to twist it around this way. We either have to go the other way, or we need to take the door off its hinges to give us another couple inches."

He strains and we twist the sofa. He gives up at last. He has to drop his end. We are stuck in the doorway.

"This doesn't have to be this hard," I say. "Let's just back it out and turn it around and it will slide right in here."

"Maybe I can get someone else to help."

"We don't really need anyone else if you are okay. We just have to come at it from a different direction."

He is insulted that I have questioned his strength. He pulls the sofa back out in a huff. We trade ends and I take it back through and it easily twists around the corner. The woman guides me to set it along the window.

"It looks good there," I say. The man is puffing. I am not even breathing heavily. It has not been much of a chore.

"Is it where you want it?" I ask. I want to be on my way.

"It's just right," she says. "Thank you so much. Arnold, give him something."

"Oh, no. I was happy to help."

Arnold springs forward, reaching into his pocket. "No, here, take something for your trouble. Here, take a quarter."

"No, thanks just the same. I was happy to help."

I skip out the front before he can press the coin on me. It has soured the whole experience. I was happy to help them, but to offer me a quarter is insulting. Maybe they are just out of touch with the times. You would tip a quarter to a shoeshine boy or a porter carrying your bag to the train.

Nothing excites us like a trip to Cincinnati to see Glenn and Lillian and their girls. Late in their marriage Lillian has given birth to a boy, Joe Dan. Glenn dotes on Joe Dan and plays ball with him. He is a lot younger than his sisters. So his dad will be his main companion growing up. But in 1948 he is still a baby. When we drive down to see them, they have moved to a house in Deer Park. After renting out in Silverton for years, they have gotten over their feeling of impermanence and decided to put down roots.

Since Glenn's mother, my Aunt Matt, is much older than my father and Glenn is her oldest boy, only ten years separate my father and Glenn in age. They are great friends and would be even closer if we lived closer to them. Now with the war over we anticipate trips down to Cincinnati more often. We take the advantage of a lull in work in the tobacco crop and go down there over the Fourth of July holiday. Clyde stays home to watch over the farm.

We are sitting in the front yard on Saturday morning and Glenn has bought a paper. He and Pop are discussing the sports section. They are both big baseball fans. Neither of them cares much for football. Glenn remarks that the St. Louis Cardinals are in town. Pop wonders if we can get tickets for the Fourth of July double-header. Glenn thinks it will be possible. It is decided that we will go.

The Fourth falls on Sunday, and I am excited over the prospect of seeing my heroes. I have just begun to keep up with baseball, and now I will get the chance to see the Reds. Pop tells Jimmy and me to drink a lot of water before leaving for the park and to take care of toiletries. We get to the ballpark early, but it is clear that there will be a big turnout. Crosley Field only holds about 30,000 spectators. We find a parking place on a back street, and Glenn tips some kids to watch the car. The neighborhood kids have been organized by the police and Reds' management to provide surveillance to cut down crime and molestation of patrons' cars. Glenn thinks the car will be safe where it is.

A big billboard on the wall outside the park is advertising Judy Garland in Meet me in St. Louis. *I think it is appropriate. Pop and Glenn stop in a bar for a quick beer. It will be more expensive once inside the park. When we get into the park on general admission tickets, we are passed around from usher to usher on where we may sit. We wind up in the upper deck on the first base side. We find four seats together only a few rows up from the walkway. People are crowding in. They anticipate a big crowd. They have roped off part of the outfield and set up seats for a few hundred more people.*

Jim plops down by Pop, and I am stuck on the end where I can't talk the game over with him. I don't mind. I am busy taking in the spectacle. The Cardinals are wearing beautiful blue uniforms. I don't find out until later that the home team always wears white and the visitors are in some shade of gray. The Cardinals are only a year away from having won the World Series. They still have Country

Slaughter and Terry Moore from that team and Stan Musial, their young phenom.

I take in the color. It is just as Waite Hoyt has described it over the radio. There is the terrace, the small elevated hill running up to the wall, the laundry where balls hit over the left field fence fall, and Grand Avenue that runs behind the rest of the outfield. Ewell Blackwell is coming off the disabled list and will pitch the first game. The year before he had been within one inning of pitching back-to-back no-hitters. But he is sore-armed this year and has been struggling. His fans still give him a big hand and his sidearm delivery is something to see. I just want the games to be good ones. And the first one is. Although Blackwell can't last, the Reds outslug the Cardinals 8-6. Johnny Wyrostek, my favorite, hits a couple home runs and Hank Sauer who has been whacking them out right along for the Reds, has another.

We are cheered by the Reds' efforts and the four of us retire to the restroom where Pop and Glenn get rid of the beer they have drunk. We go back to our seats refreshed and Pop treats Jim and me to cokes. A row of black fans above is partying and we are kept busy passing beer up to them. Finally, Pop says he won't pass anymore. He is trying to watch the game. The vendor gets Jim and me to do it.

In the second game Harry "the Cat" Brecheen shuts down the Reds. He is the fastest pitcher I have ever seen. We stay around till the ninth inning to see Hank Sauer get one more bat and he comes through with a homer, but the Reds have lost 8-1.

The next morning Glenn and Pop get a paper to read about the games and the Red Sox game in which they have had a 14-run inning. It says that 29,504 people have attended the Reds' game. It seemed like more. I cut the account of the game out of the paper and keep it for years. Then it gets misplaced somehow. It doesn't matter. The memory of it stays with me. I can always picture the park while listening to other accounts. I wish I could hear the day games somehow while I am in the tobacco field. Later, when cheap transistor radios become available, I think how I would like to have had one in those days.

Pop (in the canteen) and his son, Adrian, have a World Series pool. You put in a dollar and pick how many runs you think will be scored during the series. Brooklyn is the National League champions once again. I hate them. But I am smug that the Yankees will whip them in the series as they have always done in the past. The Yankees have Mickey Mantle, Yogi Berra, Hank Bauer, Billy Martin, and Whitey Ford. Next year when I am in Washington rooting for the Senators, I am going to go out and watch the Yankees play.

Adrian is pretty sneaky about the pool. He allows everyone to select the number of runs they think will be scored. You can choose the same number as someone else, but it means you will have to split the pot if the number comes up. It is considered to be bad form. Most people just take the next number closest to what they think it will be. Some of the secretaries just pull a number out of the hat. Some of the guys take a more scientific approach basing their choice on a six-game series with an average of six or seven runs per game. I don't bet. I am saving my money for Washington.

Adrian waits until minutes before the first game starts and the pool closes. He takes a number one lower than the previous lowest and another one higher than the previous high. Apparently this has worked for him sometime in the past. If you get several well-pitched games, the aggregate runs scored could be a low total. But by the third game they have surpassed the run total he selected on the low end. He still has a chance on the high end for it appears that they are going the full seven games.

We gather in the canteen throughout periods of the afternoon to see how the games are proceeding. I never knew there were so many baseball fans around. As far as I know no major leagues games are broadcast into Louisville. Of course, the series is on national radio. There are other radios secreted around the plant where I can duck in to catch the scores. The Yankees are going for their fifth consecutive World Series win. People are starting to think old Casey Stengel is some kind of baseball genius.

The Dodgers have a pretty good team too. They have won the pennant by 13 games over the new Milwaukee Braves which have just moved from Boston. They have Roy Campanella, Jackie Robinson, Duke Snyder, Carl Erskine, and Don Newcombe. And most of all they have Preacher Roe who has been 11-3. Everyone says this is going to be their year at last.

The series is hotly contested, but by the end the Yankees have taken it in six games. Weak hitting Billy Martin has killed the Dodgers by batting .500 and with eight RBI's. His last hit wins the last game in the last of the ninth. A number of us are listening in the canteen when the game concludes. The Dodgers have gone down in defeat again. The hated Yankees prevail once again. And Adrian contributes his two dollars to Norm Snyder who has carefully worked out the probable number of runs based on a six-game series.

* * *

Lynwood Roe with 1947 Dodge (1953)

* * *

Chapter 19

The letter comes telling me to report to the Washington Field Office in the Old Post Office on Pennsylvania Avenue on the second day of November. It is just over two weeks away. I barely have time to give my two-week's notice. I tell Mr. Gerlach on Friday so he will have an extra weekend to advertise the position. Then I have to think about the move that I will be making,

I have accumulated a lot of stuff in my room in Louisville. I have brought my basketball and Clyde's radio. I have sent Juanita's phonograph player back to her, but I still have some records. I have bought some clothing and I have both the old pressboard suitcase and my little gym bag. I will have to take some winter clothing with me when I go. And I will be wearing white shirts and ties at work, so I have to transport my suit and sport coats.

I decide I had better take a trip to the farm to take some of my stuff back and leave it there. Then, when I leave for real in two weeks, I will pack the essential things that I need. I will take the suitcase with me to Washington and a big shopping bag with the rest of my stuff. Once I get on the bus in Cincinnati, I will not have to transfer again.

When I get to the farm, Mom, Clyde, and Colleen can hardly believe it when I tell them I am going to Washington to work for the FBI. They knew I was likely to follow Juanita up there, but Mom at least was hoping I would stay close by.

"Why don't you come back here? We would give you part of the crop."

How can I tell her that I don't like farm life? It is something I can get nostalgic about, but I don't want to make my life here.

"I'm not cut out to be a farmer. And the crop is not big enough to share three ways."

"Clyde has a lot of trouble getting help to get it in the barn and stripped."

"I know. But I can't help out. I want to go to Washington."

"When will you get back?"

"Well, certainly not as often as when I was in Louisville, but I'll probably make it in a couple times every year. I'll come down on the bus, or maybe I'll get a car when I get up there."

"I knew you would follow that girl up there. Are you going to get married?"

"I don't know. We don't have any plans to do it anytime soon. I'm not thinking about that. I just want to get my new job started."

"Have you got a place to stay?"

"Not yet. The FBI may help me find something."

She is suspicious that I may move in with Juanita. She doesn't know how the FBI meddles in their employees' lives and how they will not permit anything of this kind.

Clyde thinks that I will not stay up there long. He thinks I will return to the area, if not the farm. He notes that Geneva and Odell have both left and returned after a short time away. True, they are now in Cincinnati, but it is not that far away. We have other relatives down there. It is only a two-hour trip from the farm.

"What will they pay you?" he asks.

When I went to Louisville he was highly critical of my lowly mailboy wage. I tell him I will be making $2,750 a year with the FBI. It is a government GS-2. It is a lot better than the $1,800 I made at the paint company.

"Everything will be higher up there," he warns.

"I guess. But I don't take much to live on. I saved money while I was in Louisville and I was making much less."

"Geneva and Odell never save anything."

I think of Sherman who is always trading cars and buying the latest gadgets. It seems like they are enjoying their money.

"I'm sure I will have to tighten my belt for a while. But I can live within my means."

"Stay out of debt. Don't buy on time. Easy credit gets people in debt and they never get out."

"Don't worry." It's the same advice Pop always gave out. But people have to buy on time to get a start. That's how Geneva and Sherman got their furniture and Odell and Opal theirs. Anyway, I'll be in Washington where nobody knows me. Who would give me credit there?

Pop dies at the old Massie Memorial Hospital in Paris on Thursday evening. Aunt Naomi is with him when he dies. She comes by the house late at night to tell us. Jimmy and I are in bed. We feign sleep. We don't want to get up and join the chaos downstairs. Opal, Odell, Geneva, and Aunt Naomi are all downstairs to comfort our mother. We talk lowly about it in bed. We have been expecting it, but we know our lives are going to be very different from now on.

On Friday morning we go to the funeral home. Jimmy, Colleen, and I don't have much to say in the funeral arrangements. Mom chooses the songs that had been sung at Robert and Lloyd's funerals. We are burying Pop in Carlisle Cemetery. I had thought that he would want to be buried near his parents at Mt. Tabor, but Aunt Naomi said it was his last wish to be laid in Carlisle. She already has her plot there. I wonder if she invented her deathbed conversation with him to influence the family.

Mom wants to hold a wake for Pop. The undertaker says that it has fallen out of custom in the last few years, but she is insistent. It is early August and the undertaker worries about the effects of the heat on the body. We have a viewing of the body on Friday night and relatives come in from all over. The room is piled with hothouse flowers. There are sprays of gladioluses everywhere. After a while I start to associate their smell with death.

On Saturday afternoon the body arrives at the farm. They put the casket on a catafalque in the living room. They open the casket and put a thin fine veil across to the lid to dim his features. They worry that during the night his face will darken. People wander into the room to sit in respectful silence. I am not sure what the object of the wake is. In the kitchen the women are cooking away and tons of food is being prepared.

By late evening some of people have gone home or to the houses of relatives close by. Others take up the vigil. We kids are told to go on to bed. The funeral on Sunday will be a trying experience. We are in bed and up early. I go back into the living room. I don't look too closely at the body. Louis Kirkpatrick and Perry Brown are sitting with Pop. Louis is a quiet man and gives me a friendly smile. Perry has nodded off from fatigue. I somehow guess that we are supposed to be alert in the company of the corpse, so I remain with Louis. Wynona Brown comes in to ask the men if they want some coffee. She sees Perry asleep and shakes him angrily. He lurches awake and is apologetic. Some others come in to take our places. We adjourn to the kitchen to eat once more.

It is going to be a hot, sunny day. We speculate on the number of people that will turn out. We are glad we could do this on Sunday. Everybody, including us, will need to be in their tobacco on Monday to get it housed. Everything has stopped while his friends and family pay their respects to Willie Roe. Some of them have come back to the house to see the morticians load the casket back into the hearse to go back to the funeral home. They want to refrigerate the body for a while since the casket will be open again during the service.

The family sits in a little vestibule off to the side of the chapel. We listen to the preacher saying good things about Pop. He didn't know *him. Aunt Naomi said that he accepted Jesus Christ on his last night, but I am a doubter. He has never expressed any religious thought. But he probably attended church when he was a boy. Who knows what goes through a man's mind at the end?*

At the graveside the American Legion holds a service. Elva Kendall, the commander, gives another tribute. I think he is much better than the preacher. The honor guard fires off three volleys and "Taps" is played. We walk away from the grave. Mom is desolate. I see my cousins looking pityingly at us. Pop is the first of his family of brothers and sisters to die. It occurs to me that I will, in my turn, be attending many of their funerals.

I awake at morning sudden and quick like a bloom bursting forth. I am happy to face the day. It brings me a day closer to my departure to Washington. Anybody is happy who is about to fulfill his fondest ambition. Since I visited the FBI on our Senior trip I have wanted to go back up there and work for the organization. Now all my dreams are about to be realized. Several fortunate circumstances have come together for me to make this possible. I would never have thought to apply if Juanita hadn't had her contact with them at the end of her school year. And what if she had brushed it off? What if it had not appealed to her? She would have dropped it and I would never have had my conduit to their employment office. So I couldn't take the credit wholly to myself for promoting this turn of events. But then, it couldn't be said that I had just fallen into the position. My good schoolwork, the high regard that I had established with my teachers and neighbors, and the cunning way I had dealt with the application and medical examination made me feel as though I had earned the rewards and was entitled to be elated at my success.

I go in to tell Mr. Gerlach. He is busy at something else, but he puts it aside. I present it as a fait accompli, so he doesn't even attempt to talk me out of it or suggest that I might want something else around the plant.

"You have been the best mail clerk I can ever remember us having," he said.

"Thanks. I've tried. I know I screwed up some. I finally got the hang of it. It just takes some time to catch on."

"I thought you might want to stay on with us. I was thinking the other day about where we might put you."

Why hadn't he said something? I am curious even though it is too late now.

"Where would that have been?" I asked.

"Probably down in the Orders Department. I asked the people over in Personnel about your application when you came in. They said you did very well on the examination they give everybody."

The Orders Department is where Doug Hopkins, one of the earlier mailboys, works, so I know that it is possible that he is not just saying it.

"Well, that's nice to know. But I am committed to the FBI now."

"Yes, we can't seem to hold on to good people," he smiles. Madelaine is taking it all in. She will spread the news all over the plant.

"It's good of you to say so. Hold the job for me. If I screw up at the FBI, maybe they will fire me, and I will come back here, hat in hand."

"Ridiculous. You'll do fine there. We're glad you're moving on to something else you like better. We're sorry you are going, and we will miss you."

I think he is going to rise from the desk and shake my hand, but he turns to practical matters.

"Now when is your last day? We've got to go out and hunt up a new clerk and get him in here for you to train."

"I'll need to leave on the last day of the month. The day before Halloween."

"That's good. We'll get an ad in the paper on Sunday and again on Monday. We'll see what we can turn up."

He seems to be clicking off in his mind what he needs to do to fill my position.

"Stop in Personnel and tell Mr. Phillips. He will be the one calling in the ad. And let him know you have already told me. I suppose you will be wanting to be paid on that Friday?"

"If it's convenient." Of course I want to be paid. I'll need the money. I can't stop by for my money later.

"Madelaine will have it ready for you. We'll assume that you are leaving with the other staff on that day and won't have to figure in any overtime."

"It's been swell working with you all. I'm sorry to make this extra work for everybody."

Madelaine smiles. She reminds me of some of my teachers who have patiently watched over me in my younger years.

"Woodie, I knew you were destined for bigger things," she says. "Get on up there to Washington and get that mess cleaned up."

The year Pop dies it looks like it will be a grim Christmas for the family. Pop didn't leave a will. He expected his estate to pass on to Mom, but by Kentucky law she is only entitled to one-seventh. Odell and Geneva want their shares. The farm will have to be sold to satisfy them. Of course, Mom will have the shares of us younger children in trust, but until the farm is sold, she can't get at much of the money. She is given an advance, but we have to make it last.

We can't waste money on a tree, but Jim and I find one on the back of Mr. Maffett's farm and cut it and drag it home on the sled. It is a scruffy affair and remains that way despite our efforts to decorate it gaily. Colleen is unhappy and wants us to go buy one. But we get used to it and it looks even better when some presents are added under it.

Geneva and Odell and their families get in for Christmas and Mom finds a way to buy the things she needs to prepare the Christmas feast. The dearth of presents makes those we do get seem dearer. We build a cheery fire in the usually unused fireplace. We burn cedar logs for their scent and listen to the Christmas shows on the radio.

Before we can get back into school, a big storm blows through and drifts the roads and closes the school. It is followed by a freezing rain that makes everything slick and drives the animals into the barn. It makes for good sleigh-riding on the hill in front of our house. Afterwards, we come in half-frozen from sledding and warm our hands on Mom's coal-fired cookstove and eat popcorn and drink hot cocoa.

We take our tractor and break the road through to Headquarters so we can get supplies at the store. We go up there in the evening and watch wrestling on the television. Jimmy always drives with Clyde and me sitting on the two fenders. A road grader finally comes down the valley clearing the road and a rain blows through completing the melting process. We are able to get out and go to town and attend the movies and catch up on what is happening in the Republic Pictures serial that is playing.

Back in school my classmates are talking about their holidays and showing off the finery they have received. Some of them are ecstatic because their families have bought themselves new televisions for entertainment. Miss Botts thinks it would be cute to go around the room and have each student tell what they have received. I don't want to play the game and am ready to make up several things when catcalls from some of my unruly classmates convinces her that she will have to terminate the game. Somehow I feel that despite not getting many presents, it has been a good Christmas and one I'll remember.

Richard Davis is hired on as my replacement. He is older and married. He worries about whether or not the job will pay well enough for him to support his family. He has a young daughter. He says that he is a preacher in the Wesleyan Methodist Church.

They pay him something, but I gather not much. I think he has been the only applicant for the job. He seems totally unsuitable for it.

I take him around and introduce him to everyone as Paul had done for me. I try to take him over to have lunch with my crowd, but he says he needs to get his sermon prepared. His wife has fixed him a sandwich. He stays back in the switchboard room and eats and looks through his Bible and makes notes. None of the people around the plant like him. He is rather sullen and untalkative. It would seem that a preacher would be more outgoing to people. Some of the women say that he gives them the creeps. Bev, who stays late on the switchboard in the evenings, says that she will not stay with him. I wonder how they are going to solve the impasse. I encourage him to talk in the afternoon when we are getting the mail ready to go out. I hope that she will warm to him.

I think that with the Reverend Richard Davis and Bertha, the plant is taking on a decidedly weird slant. But that is not my worry. Maybe if I could have given them more notice they would have come up with a better replacement. I always introduce him as the new mail clerk rather than mailboy. I remembered how down I felt when I was being referred to as a mailboy. It somehow seemed to be a diminution of my position.

Although I have never stopped in at the drugstore on any of my mail runs, I think that I will treat Richard Davis as Paul did for me earlier. We drop in on our way back from the post office one day and I buy him a soda. He thanks me, but as we leave, he asks if we aren't reimbursed for bus fare if we wait and catch a bus back to the office from the Post Office? I tell him we are so-entitled. It has never crossed my mind to do so. I walk everywhere I can. So the next day I send him to the bank and Post Office on his own, while I buzz around and talk to some people. He shows up back a little later than I usually do. He has waited for a bus.

Virginia seems a little antsy handing him over the bag for the bank deposit. But he has obviously been bonded the same as I was when I came to Jones-Dabney. At mornings the guys stopping to give us a ride seem surprised to see Richard. They give him a grudging welcome. I wonder if they will continue to pick him up at morning. On my last day, Friday, I leave it to him to pick up the mail, and I meet him at the office. He is late. He says that he caught the first bus that came along. I tell him that the drivers at Jones-Dabney just don't recognize him yet and soon they'll be picking him up before the bus arrives.

By my last day the glow of the new job has dimmed for Richard. He talks openly about looking for something else. He does not think he can make it on the salary he is getting. The long hours depress him because it keeps him from his church work. He has had spats with his wife who wants to take a job to supplement their income. He doesn't want her working. He is kind of old-fashioned or just chauvinistic. Maybe there is something in the Bible about wives keeping the house and raising the kids and not working. I think that it is not my problem. I have handed it over to him as best I could. He is on his own and he and Jones-Dabney will have to work out their differences.

Near the end of my Junior year in high school we take some class trips that brighten the school year. Two of these are day trips on a county school bus. And we arrive back at the school so late that everyone has to make arrangements to get home from there. In one case I am able to hop off the bus as it passes near my road and walk home. The other time Billy Mattox takes me home in his pickup truck that he has left at school.

Our big trip is to Mammoth Cave for three days and two nights. The class has sold refreshments at some of the basketball games, and we have raised money in a number of other ways, including a class play.

But we still have to put some money of our own into it. I hate to ask Mom for it, but I don't want to miss the trip.

We ride down Route 68 with Huddie Snapp, our janitor, driving the bus. Huddie is going to be one of the chaperones. Miss Botts has brought her sister along for another. Miss Botts wants us to stop and visit the Monastery of Gethsemane in Loretto. We want to get on to Mammoth Cave. I get Huddie to pretend that he doesn't see the sign to turn off. He is apologetic to Miss Botts. She says it is all right.

On the road to Mammoth Cave several wildcat cave owners have set up little booths occupied by agents dressed as park rangers. We have been warned by all to ignore these people. They will try to redirect us to the caves they own nearby. I get Huddie to stop over the objections of my classmates. I want to hear what they have to say. The man makes a pitch for his cave. I ask him how big it is and if we will get a discount rate on a large group. He gives us a couple brochures, and I assure him that if we have some time left over we will stop by to see his cave. He thinks he has lured some potential tourists until the basketball players give him a horse-laugh as we pull away.

Some of my classmates are disappointed in the old hotel, but I think it is swell. We boys are four to a room. There is a lot of horseplay and it is obvious that the Botts sisters are going to have their hands full. We will be lucky not to get thrown out. My classmates are using the roof of the long front porch to crawl from one room to the next.

But no one wants to go to bed. There is a jukebox in the front lobby and it plays continuously. Some of the other guests are dancing. Some of our girls dance with each other. None of the boys in the class know how to dance. "How High the Moon" by Les Paul and Mary Ford is the favorite song they are playing. We finally go off to bed. We know that we are taking the seven-mile all-day tour in the morning. We find out later that Miss Botts has spent much of the night in her housecoat in the hallway stopping the traffic between the rooms. She does not go with us on the tour. She sends her sister and Huddie. I am paired with Doug Clay. Each pair of walkers shares a lantern.

There is another class from Ravenna High School. There is a gorgeous girl named Agnes. I ask some of her classmates about her. They say she is stuck up. I try a time or two to talk to her. But she stays in the company of her class's chaperones. I give up on her and walk with Ann Collins for a while. I am never sure if Ann and I have a thing or not. I think she likes me, but maybe she is put off by my small stature.

Later when we stop at Joyland Park in Lexington on the way back, Ann and I ride some of the rides together. But it is all Dutch. I don't have money to spend on girls. And if I had hit it off with Agnes, how could we have ever seen each other again?

Chapter 20

Everyone knows now that I am leaving. It is gratifying to get so many well-wishes and expressions of friendship. The lunchtime crowd wants to hear all about the FBI. They think it sounds like I am going off to do something glamorous instead of taking a plain clerking job. I don't try to make it sound glamorous. I know it will be a pedestrian sort of job. But an opportunity may arise to make something more of it.

Jimmy Andrews makes it seem like I am leaving a big void in the basketball team. Since I have been called to report to the bureau I have not attended the most recent practices. I gather he is having a hard time getting commitments from all his mercenaries and the other guys on the team are resisting bringing in outsiders who will shorten their playing time. They are willing to forego the championship if it means they will get to play more themselves.

On the last day I am told to report to the Accounting Section just after lunch. The ladies up there have put together a little party. They have blown up balloons and penciled a sign that reads "Good Luck, Woodie." They have bought me some small presents, but they rightly perceive that I am in more need of some cash. They hand over 25 dollars that they have collected. I am touched. They want me to say something. I stammer out my thanks and tell them how I have enjoyed working with them. Pauline is there. She was one of the first people I met at Jones-Dabney. It seems strange that I will be gone and she will still be reporting in each day and working at her desk in the back of the Accounting room just as always.

Only Pamela Brown has stood with me. The other ladies watch from their desks. After a while they go back to work. I don't know what else to say. I thank them again and leave. I think that I should have gone around and said goodbye to each one individually. But there are a few in the room whom I never got to know. I won't be able to come back with Richard on his last mail run. I have said my goodbyes to them. I send him off on the last mail run of the day, and I slip out and go around the plant and say goodbye to everyone. To Lorna Leibowitz and Walter and Bruce Abell. To the people in Personnel. To Pop and Adrian. To Bertha, Irma, Doris, and Nadine. To Mrs. Stevenson. When I get back to the switchboard room, Aggie is preparing to leave. I tell her goodbye. I don't ask what Bev has decided about Richard Davis.

Madelaine comes out of the office and gives me my last paycheck. I will cash it on the way back to my room. She and Mr. Gerlach tell me goodbye. People are lining up to punch out on the clock. I walk down the line shaking hands and saying goodbye. The ladies from Accounting are there so I say goodbye again and thank them for their gifts. The girls in the front office file out. The Joans say goodbye. Sassy Nancy Higgins kisses me on the cheek and tells me she will miss me. Virginia follows last and kisses me as well. I tell her I hope she will have a good life if I don't see her again.

It is done. My ties with Jones-Dabney are about cut. Some people like Norm are still flitting around. It seems unnatural to be leaving so early in the day. I check once again with Richard to see if he has any problems. He is metering the mail. It seems to be running smoothly. There is nothing left to do except say goodbye to him and to Bev.

I leave by the front door and say goodbye to the guard who has watched everyone check out. Some kids are out front. I notice them sometimes when I bring the mail out in the evening. I ignore them every time they are there. In past times I was carrying the mail over to the mailbox to make sure it was posted on time. Today I am carrying nothing. I look over at the kids as I pass. They are a little older than I thought. Maybe high school kids almost my age. I smile at them.

"Hello, stuck-up," a girl says.

In school classes usually have a different homeroom teacher or sponsor every year. The Juniors get Miss Botts and everybody dreads it. She is the math teacher and hopelessly old-fashioned. She drives an old 1934 Ford to school every day. She chaperones us on our Mammoth Cave trip and she is a good sport about it even though some of my classmates give her some bad moments in the hotel.

She surprises us by throwing a party for us at her home at the end of the school year. She lives with her aged father and an unmarried sister just outside Carlisle. I have no way to get there, so I tell her I cannot come. She tells me to come home with her and I can help her get the place set up for the party. Then Billy Mattox will take me home.

I am something of her pet. I am good in math. And better still, I am quiet and studious in class and don't give her a hard time. I think I have gotten on her good side in freshman study hall when I always got my homework done and prowled the library shelves devouring books. I don't particularly like math and algebra, but they aren't a mystery to me as they seem to be to some of my classmates. Beyond basic application of arithmetic skills, I don't see the need of being able to solve complex formulas.

All my classmates show up for the party. It is nearly the end of the school year. We have bonded on our trips to Mammoth Cave and High Bridge. I still haven't found a girlfriend though. We play

211

parlor games. And Miss Botts has trouble keeping her father out of the room. He wants to take part in the proceedings.

Eventually we get into kissing games. It was inevitable that the other simple-minded things such as drawing slips of paper with little tasks on them would wear thin. We get the chairs in a circle and the girls sit down with the boys behind them. We have about the same number of girls as boys in the class. One of the chairs is empty. The boy slyly winks at a girl. If the girl can slip away she comes to the empty chair. If the boy behind her sees the wink and catches her before she can slip away, she has to kiss him. You can tell which boys certain girls like because they allow themselves to be caught and kissed.

Then it is time to switch places and the boys take the chairs with the girls behind them. I am seldom winked at and then the girl usually lets me escape. Still, I get a few kisses. I feel sorry for Wayne Spegal. He is so ugly that I think that the girls must be feeling pity for him when they catch him to kiss him. But he is enjoying himself hugely. It is a special night. I wonder if the Misses Botts are reliving some of their girlhood memories.

Next day Miss Botts asks if Billy Mattox and I will go back over to her house in his pickup truck and retrieve a couple cases of soda pop that were left over from the party. She wants to return them to the school lunchroom and get her money back. She trusts us to not lollygag but to get right back to school. We have all that pop with us and no way to open the bottles. Billy stops on the hill just west of town and hooks a bottle under the dashboard of his pickup truck. He gives it a sharp rap and the bottle cap pops off. We revel in sipping the warm orange pop on the trip back to school.

Youth is a wonderful thing. There is nothing else like in our lives. But the young who have it hardly know what to do with it. They do not realize that it will only be with them for a short time and then gone forever. They chafe at the restrictions. They decry that they have not accumulated wealth at this point, or have absorbed life experience that enables them to attain occupations that interest them. They want fame, but have yet to build the reputations that will bring them honor. They want to apply themselves, but their minds and energies are spent on lustful thoughts and sensual pursuits.

A young man is not able to use this youth – this vigor, this strength, this happy time – to achieve the life he desires. He does not envy other youths – he yearns for and hungers after the accomplishment of older men – those who have reached their pinnacles of power and fame. He does not know how to apply himself. In his pursuits he does not realize until too late that he has squandered this time. He has consciously tried to put it behind him, and when he has done so, there is no getting it back. And finally, down the road of his life, he is left with the memories of this time. The ashes of his youth. The pressed petals of life and love's first bloom.

Neither have I used this time well. The year on the farm has been wasted. I should have tried to get into a college by working to pay my tuition or trying to get help of some kind. Even a stint in the armed forces to get the GI bill would have probably paid later dividends. But I am not pulled toward the military and am pulled away by Juanita. Now the job in Washington may provide the opportunity for me to get my life back on track. I will give it my best. I know of no other way. Even in my low mailboy position I have done a good job. In my summer in Louisville I have absorbed the sights and sounds and added to my life experience. I come away a better person. A changed person in some ways. I am confident that I can meet any challenge. Given a fair chance I can perform at any job that others can do.

I have enjoyed my summer in Louisville. I have shed some of my farm boy aspects. My demeanor has taken on a cosmopolitan taint. I can go into a fine restaurant and order. I have a good taste in clothes, although my purse constrains me to be selective. I can mix with and talk to a variety of people with varied backgrounds. Conversations can center on a multitude of subjects – not just weather and crops and livestock. My summer's experience will stand me in good stead for whatever comes later. Wherever my steps lead me.

But I will not realize until later that I have brought to the experience the full vigor of optimistic youth. Never again will I be as fresh-faced and cherry-cheeked. Never again will I have the spring to my step and the lilt to my heart. I take a lot away from Louisville because I brought a lot to it. It is the happy coincidence of meeting a town at its best when I am at my best. A confluence of youth and a city that sung a siren's song.

We Seniors practice marching in for Baccalaureate and graduation. We have been waiting for this for twelve years so we don't mind the repetition. Miss Stump, the music teacher, is in charge. She lines us up and has us come in over and over. We stand around and talk. We are out of class and enjoying it.

We enter the gym in two lines from tallest to shortest. Jimmy Judge and I have a dispute over who is the shortest. We finally stand back to back and I am adjudged to be taller. So he will have to march in last. I am stupid. If I had let him go in first I would have been the first one to receive my diploma at the new school.

So instead of marching with Bonnie Richie whom everybody has always wanted to pair me up with in school, I march with Fay Letcher. I have come out of my shell near graduation and am having a lot of fun with my classmates. I am jealous of Bonnie and Alma Dean Hudnall who give the valedictorian and salutatorian speeches. I think I am smarter, but I have always had to help in the crops in the fall and in the evenings after school, and cannot always get my homework completed.

On my Senior trip I have been such a card that my classmates name me class poet. I have composed poems about all my classmates and at Class Night I get up and read them. I am a great hit. Huddie Snapp corners me and wants to read what I have written about him. He is the janitor and has a jealous wife who thinks all the girls are after him. He is afraid that I will read something that will set her off. But he is placated by my sentimental poem and okays it. I try not to embarrass anybody, but a lot of them are inside jokes and meaningful only to us students.

After two weeks of rehearsal, Baccalaureate is a disaster. Harvey Wilson and Ruby Smith lead us in and, despite being rehearsed over and over, they march in much too slow. We are nearly an hour getting in. Miss Stump is exhausted from pounding out "Pomp and Circumstance" on the piano. The next day she is all over them about their slow pace. On graduation night they practically run up the aisle.

Mom, Clyde, and Colleen attend from my family. None of my other relatives have come to watch. We each get ten tickets down close to the stage for our families. I give the rest of mine away to my classmates so they won't go to waste.

Also attending my graduation is Juanita Caswell who I have found out is sweet on me. Just today I have asked her to go with me to the Junior/Senior weenie roast at Blue Licks on Monday, the last day of school. I wonder where that will lead just as I wonder what will become of me now that I have finished school.

I rise early and dress. I have told the Shaws goodbye the night before. I have taken a bath last night and don't have to wake people up banging around. I have packed the old pressboard suitcase, and it is full going back. I have a shopping bag too and Clyde's radio is in there with some phonograph records and everything wrapped in shirts and pants to cushion it. I have the box of toffee that commemorated Queen Elizabeth's coronation.

The toffee is almost gone. I use the box to place odds and ends in.

I look around my room for the last time. On these cold nights in late October I have to sleep with the window closed. The limbs that whispered me to sleep in the summer have lost their leaves. The room looks warm and friendly and familiar. But I have to move on.

I slip down the stairs quietly and leave my key on the mail table. The door latches behind me. I start for the Fourth Street bus stop. Sixth Street would be closer for me to reach and would drop me closer to the Greyhound bus station, but the Fourth Street buses run more often, and I have a schedule to meet. All the things I see walking across seem to be a farewell look. Central Park and the opulent houses along the street I have passed many times. The cross streets and intersections I know as well as the fences on the farm in Nicholas County.

I am early at the station. The bus to Lexington has not yet pulled in. I stand on the street and look up and down Broadway. It is hard to believe that less than six months ago I walked out of this selfsame station and stood in this very spot wondering where in this now-familiar city I could find a room for the night. I look out toward the west where I had walked with my pressboard suitcase that I clutched again now, and saw the place where the Negro bum had hailed me and took me along to find me quarters. And the other way where I had finally walked back to the YMCA at Second Street where I spent my first night in sleepless bewilderment at being away from the farm and in the big city. Somewhere beyond the row of buildings across the street is the river and lower Fourth Street where I have spent many pleasant hours alone browsing the stores or with Juanita. And behind me some ten blocks or so is the plant at Jones-Dabney pretty much vacated for the weekend, but ready to spring to life on Monday morning. Come to life without Woodie Roe who had been a good mailboy and had helped keep the wheels of commerce turning.

No, I won't be there. The others – Aggie and Mr. Gerlach, and Virginia and the Joans, and Norm Snyder, and Pop and Adrian, and Bertha will be going on with their lives in the same old way. Will they remember me at all? Will they pause at their work from time to time and think, "I wonder what Woodie is doing now up there with all the other G-Men today?"

The bus pulls into the bay and I load aboard with the others. With the ride into the farm I will be on buses for about twenty-four hours this weekend. We will drive through towns and see kids out trick-or-treating. I will see the West Virginia hills that I had once passed through on an overnight train. I will see sleepy little mountain towns and fog-enshrouded streams. I will see the monuments and federal buildings that are shown on the television news every night.

I will enter a different world and a new life. I have shed my cocoon.

* * *

Washington D.C., December 1953

* * *